The Enriched Reading

Edited by

D. Sudha Rani
HOD, H&M
Malla Reddy Engineering College (Autonomous)
Secunderabad
Telangana

Editor – Acquisitions: Kaushal Jajware
Editor—Production: G. Sharmilee

ISBN 978-93-325-5688-1

First Impression, 2016

Published by Pearson India Education Services Pvt. Ltd,
CIN: U72200TN2005PTC057128.

Head Office: 15th Floor, Tower-B, World Trade Tower, Plot No. 1, Block-C, Sector 16, Noida 201 301, Uttar Pradesh, India.

Registered Office: 4th floor, Software Block, Elnet Software City, TS 140 Block 2 & 9, Rajiv Gandhi Salai, Taramani, Chennai - 600 113, Tamil Nadu, Fax: 080-30461003, Phone: 080-30461060, Website: in.pearson.com
Email: companysecretary.india@pearson.com

Compositor: Map Systems

Digitally Printed in India by Repro Books Limited, Thane in the year of 2019.

Contents

Introduction *v*

Acknowledgements *vii*

About the Editor and Contributors *vii*

Speeches

1. Grammar of Anarchy 3
2. I Have a Dream: An Independent, Developed and Strong India 13
3. Nobel Lecture 21
4. Life is not Milk and Roses 29
5. Stay Hungry, Stay Foolish 37

Short Stories

6. Death of a Hero 45
7. The Doctor's Word 55
8. The Ultimate Weapon 63
9. The Open Window 75
10. Once There was a King 83

Literary Credits *93*

Introduction

The Enriched Reading is a compilation of a few inspiring speeches (adaptations) and thought-provoking short stories. Undergraduate students need to participate in nation building, enrich their knowledge and develop their social sensibility. The adaptation of speeches is carefully done with a focus on inspiration, education and communication. The selected speakers are the constitution maker, Dr Ambedkar; the most influential President among youth of India, A.P.J. Abdul Kalam; the most renowned scientist from India, C.V. Raman; the child rights activist from India who shared Nobel peace prize in 2014, Kailash Satyarthi and the inspirational technocrat, Steve Jobs. All these great personalities speak about who is a good citizen and how can you assess whether or not you are a good citizen. They also give you a sense of direction and a sense of responsibility towards your society and country. The language used and the delivery will certainly inspire you.

The short stories selected include stories which would appeal your human element and give you joy and enrich your human sensibility. These short stories are taken from Indian perspective to establish a strong emotional and cultural connect. Besides, they represent our journey of continuous struggle between justice and injustice (The Real Hero), our predicament as dependents (The Ultimate Weapon), the importance of a doctors' word (The Doctor's Word), the difference between reality and fantasy (The Open Window) and the beauty of childhood and the innocence (Once There Was a King).

The main objective of *The Enriched Reading* is to inculcate a habit of reading, analysing and re-presenting an idea. The exercises at the end of the each chapter help to make you analyse and re-present the ideas of the speech/short story. The focus is on developing the vocabulary and reading skills. So the teachers are advised to make the students read the speech/short story on their own. Time should be utilized not only for working out the exercises given at the end of each section but also for supplementing the exercises with authentic materials of a similar kind, for example, from newspaper articles, advertisements, promotional material, etc. However, the focus of this book is on fostering ideas, practice of language skills and skill development.

Acknowledgements

The Enriched Reading is a reality because of the hard work of a group of English language teachers who share a common thought to include literature in English language education at undergraduate level. We thank everyone who supported *us* through this journey. We will be pleased to receive constructive criticism from both learners and our fellow English teachers across the country.

About the Editor and Contributors

The book *The Enriched Reading* is the result of a team work done by a group of English language teachers of Malla Reddy Engineering College (Autonomous), Dhulapally, Secunderabad. This team includes D. Sudha Rani, B. Vijay Kumar, K.S. Rajashree, Keerthi Krishnamurthy, P. Srujana, Nasreen Begum, A. Madhavilatha, Meenakshi Dhondi.

Speeches

Chapter One

Grammar of Anarchy

Dr B.R. Ambedkar

Bhimrao Ambedkar was born on 14th April 1891 in Madhya Pradesh. His parents, Bhimabai Sakpal and Ramji, hailed from the Hindu Mahar caste, which was viewed as 'untouchable' by the upper class. Being a victim of caste discrimination and humiliation, he fought for the rights of the dalits and other socially backward classes. Dr B.R. Ambedkar is viewed as messiah of dalits and downtrodden in India.

He was the chairman of the Drafting Committee that was formed by the Constituent Assembly in 1947 to draft the constitution of independent India. He played a seminal role in the framing of the constitution. Bhimrao Ambedkar was also the first Law Minister of India in the Cabinet of Jawaharlal Nehru. For his yeoman service to the nation, he was posthumously awarded the Bharat Ratna, India's highest civilian honour, in 1990.

The following text is an excerpt from the Constituent Assembly speech by Dr B.R. Ambedkar, given on Friday, 25th November 1949. Dr Ambedkar's speech in the Constituent Assembly explains the form of the government and the constitution envisaged by the Drafting Committee.

I feel, however good a constitution may be, it is sure to turn out bad because those who are called to work it happen to be a bad lot. However bad a constitution may be, it may turn out to be good if those who are called to work it happen to be a good lot. The working of a constitution does not depend wholly upon the nature of the constitution. The constitution can provide only the organs of State such as the legislature, the executive and the judiciary. The factors on which the working of those organs of the State depend are the people and the political parties they will set up as their instruments to carry out their wishes and their politics. Who can say how the people of India and their parties will behave? Will they uphold constitutional methods of achieving their purposes or will they prefer revolutionary methods of achieving them? If they adopt the revolutionary methods, however good the constitution may be, it requires no prophet to say that it will fail. It is, therefore, futile to pass any judgement upon the constitution without reference to the part which the people and their parties are likely to play.

... my mind is so full of the future of our country that I feel I ought to take this occasion to give expression to some of my reflections thereon. On 26th January 1950, India will be an independent country (*Cheers*). What would happen to her independence? Will she maintain her independence, or will she lose it again? This is the first thought that comes to my mind. It is not that India was never an independent country. The point is that she once lost the independence she had. Will she lose it a second time? It is this thought which makes me most anxious for the future. What perturbs me greatly is the fact that not only India has once before lost her independence, but she lost it by the infidelity and treachery of some of her own people. In the invasion of Sind by Mohommed-Bin-Kasim, the military commanders of King Dahar accepted bribes from the agents of Mohommed-Bin-Kasim and refused to fight on the side of their king. It was Jaichand who invited Mohommed Ghori to invade India and fight against Prithvi Raj, and promised him the help of himself and the Solanki kings. When Shivaji was fighting for the liberation of Hindus, the other Maratha noblemen and the Rajput kings were fighting the battle on the side of Moghul emperors. When the British were trying to destroy the Sikh rulers, Gulab Singh, their principal commander sat silent and did not help to save the Sikh kingdom. In 1857, when a large part of India had declared a war of independence against the British, the Sikhs stood and watched the event as silent spectators.

Will history repeat itself? It is this thought which fills me with anxiety. This anxiety is deepened by the realization of the fact that in addition to our old enemies in the form of castes and creeds, we are going to have many political parties with diverse and opposing political creeds. Will Indians place the country above their creed or will they place creed above country? I do not know. But this much is certain that if the parties place creed above country, our independence will be put in *jeopardy* a second time and probably be lost forever. This eventuality we must all resolutely guard against. We must be determined to defend our independence with the last drop of our blood (*Cheers*).

On 26th January 1950, India would be a democratic country in the sense that India from that day would have a government of the people, by the people and for the people. The same thought comes to my mind. What would happen to her democratic constitution? Will she be able to maintain it or will she lose it again. This is the second thought that comes to my mind and makes me as anxious as the first.

It is not that India did not know what is democracy. There was a time when India was studded with republics, and even where there were monarchies, they were either elected or limited. They were never absolute. It is not that India did not know parliaments or parliamentary procedure. A study of the Buddhist *Bhikshu Sanghas* discloses that not only there were parliaments – for the *Sanghas* were nothing but parliaments – but the *Sanghas* knew and observed all the rules of parliamentary procedure known to modern times. They had rules regarding seating arrangements, rules regarding motions, resolutions, quorum, whip, counting of votes, voting by ballot, censure motion, regularization, res judicata, etc. Although these rules of parliamentary procedure were applied by the Buddha to the meetings of the Sanghas, he must have borrowed them from the rules of the political assemblies functioning in the country in his time.

This democratic system India lost. Will she lose it a second time? I do not know. But it is quite possible in a country like India – where democracy, from its long disuse, must be regarded as something quite new. There is danger of democracy giving place to dictatorship. It is quite possible for this new born democracy to retain its form but give place to dictatorship in fact. If there is a landslide, the danger of the second possibility becoming actuality is much greater.

If we wish to maintain democracy not merely in form but also in fact, what must we do? The first thing in my judgement we must do is to hold fast to constitutional methods of achieving our social and economic objectives. It means we must abandon the bloody methods of revolution. It means that we must abandon the method of civil disobedience, non-cooperation and satyagraha. When there was no way left for constitutional methods for achieving economic and social objectives, there was a great deal of justification for unconstitutional methods. But where constitutional methods are open, there can be no justification for these unconstitutional methods. These methods are nothing but the Grammar of Anarchy and the sooner they are abandoned, the better for us.

The second thing we must do is to observe the caution which John Stuart Mill has given to all who are interested in the maintenance of democracy, namely, not 'to lay their liberties at the feet of even a great man, or to trust him with power which enable him to subvert their institutions'. There is nothing wrong in being grateful to great men who have rendered life-long services to the country. But there are limits to gratefulness. As has been well said by the Irish Patriot Daniel O'Connel, no man can be grateful at the cost of his honour, no woman can be grateful at the cost of her chastity and no nation can be grateful at the cost of its liberty. This caution is far more necessary in the case of India than in the case of any other country. For in India, *Bhakti* or what may be called the path of devotion or hero-worship, plays a part in its politics unequalled in magnitude by the part it plays in the politics of any other country in the world. *Bhakti* in religion may be a road to the salvation of the soul. But in politics, *Bhakti* or hero-worship is a sure road to degradation and to eventual dictatorship.

The third thing we must do is not to be content with mere political democracy. We must make our political democracy a social democracy as well. Political democracy cannot last unless there lies at the base of it social democracy. What does social democracy mean? It means a way of life which recognizes liberty, equality and fraternity as the principles of life. These principles of liberty, equality and fraternity are not to be treated as separate items in a trinity. They form a union of trinity in the sense that to divorce one from the other is to defeat the very purpose of democracy. Liberty cannot be divorced from equality, equality cannot be divorced from liberty. Nor can liberty and equality be divorced from fraternity. Without equality, liberty would produce the supremacy of the few over the many. Equality without liberty would kill individual initiative. Without fraternity, liberty would produce the supremacy of the few over the many. Equality without liberty would kill individual initiative. Without fraternity, liberty and equality could not become a natural course of things. It would require a constable to enforce them. We must begin by acknowledging the fact that there is complete absence of two things in Indian society. One of these is equality. On the social plane, we have in India a society based on the principle of graded inequality which we have a society in which there are some who have immense wealth as against many who live in abject poverty. On 26th January 1950, we are going to enter into a life of contradictions. In politics we will have equality, and in social and economic life we will have inequality. In politics we will be recognizing the principle of one man, one vote and one vote, one value. In our social and economic life, we shall, by reason of our social and economic structure, continue to deny the principle of one man one value. How long shall we continue to live this life of contradictions? How long shall we continue to deny equality in our social and economic life? If we continue to deny it for long, we will do so only by putting our political democracy in peril. We must remove this contradiction at the earliest possible moment or else those who suffer from inequality will blow up the structure of political democracy which this Assembly has to laboriously built up.

The second thing we are wanting in is recognition of the principle of fraternity. What does fraternity mean? Fraternity means a sense of common brotherhood of all Indians, of Indians being one people. It is the principle which gives unity and solidarity to social life. It is a difficult thing to achieve. How difficult it is can be realized from the story related by *James Bryce* in his volume on American Commonwealth about the United States of America.

The story is – I propose to recount it in the words of Bryce himself – that

'Some years ago the American Protestant Episcopal Church was occupied at its triennial Convention in revising its liturgy. It was thought desirable to introduce among the short sentence prayers, a prayer for the whole people, and an eminent New England divine proposed the words "O Lord, bless our nation". Accepted one afternoon, on the spur of the moment, the sentence was brought up next day for reconsideration, when so many objections were raised by the laity to the word "nation" as importing too definite a recognition of national unity that it was dropped, and instead there were adopted the words "O Lord, bless these United States"'.

There was so little solidarity in the United States at the time when this incident occurred that the people of America did not think that they were a nation. If the people of the United States could not feel that they were a nation, how difficult it is for Indians to think that they are a nation. I remember the days when politically minded Indians, *resented* the expression 'the people of India'. They preferred the expression 'the Indian nation'. I am of opinion that in believing that we are a nation, we are cherishing a great delusion. How can people divided into several thousands of castes be a nation? The sooner we realize that we are not as yet a nation in the social and psychological sense of the world, the better for us. For then only we shall realize the necessity of becoming a nation and seriously think of ways and means of realizing the goal. The realization of this goal is going to be very difficult – far more difficult than it has been in the United States. The United States has no caste problem. In India there are castes. The castes are anti-national. In the first place because they bring about separation in social life. They are anti-national also because they generate jealousy and antipathy between caste and caste. But we must overcome all these difficulties if we wish to become a nation in reality. For fraternity can be a fact only when there is a nation. Without fraternity, equality and liberty will be no deeper than coats of paint.

These are my reflections about the tasks that lie ahead of us. They may not be very pleasant to some. But there can be no gainsaying that political power in this country has too long been the monopoly of a few, and the many are only beasts of burden, but also beasts of prey. This monopoly has not merely deprived them of their chance of betterment, it has sapped them of what may be called the significance of life. These downtrodden classes are tired of being governed. They are impatient to govern themselves. This urge for self-realization in the downtrodden classes must not be allowed to devolve into a class struggle or class war. It would lead to a division of the House. That would indeed be a day of disaster. For, as has been well said by Abraham Lincoln, a house divided against itself cannot stand very long. Therefore the sooner room is made for the realization of their aspiration, the better for the few, the better for the country, the better for the maintenance for its independence and the better for the continuance of its democratic structure. This can only be done by the establishment of equality and fraternity in all spheres of life. That is why I have laid so much stresses on them.

I do not wish to weary the house any further. Independence is no doubt a matter of joy. But let us not forget that this independence has thrown on us great responsibilities. By independence, we have lost the excuse of blaming the British for anything going wrong. If hereafter things go wrong, we will have nobody to blame except ourselves. There is great danger of things going wrong. Times are fast changing. People, including our own, are being moved by new ideologies. They are getting tired of government by the people. They are prepared to have governments for the people and are indifferent whether it is government of the people and by the people. If we wish to preserve the constitution in which we have sought to enshrine the principle of government of the people, for the people and by the people, let us resolve not to be tardy in the recognition of the evils that lie across our path and which induce people to prefer government for the people to government by the people, nor to be weak in our initiative to remove them. That is the only way to serve the country. I know of no better.

GLOSSARY

Antipathy : A feeling of dislike; aversion
Delusion : A false belief
Devolve : Transfer; change
Enshrine : Cherish or preserve
James Bryce : A British academic and an ambassador to the United States

Jeopardy : In danger or at risk
John Stuart Mill : A British philosopher and political economist belonging to the 19th century
Infidelity : Act that lacks loyalty
Liturgy : A form of public service officially prescribed by the Church
Parliament : A representative body having supreme legislative powers within a state organization
Perturb : Make (someone) anxious, upset
Res judicata : (especially in law) A matter already adjudicated upon that cannot be raised again
Resent : Feel bitter; indignant or aggrieved
Solidarity : Unity among the same class
Studded : Competed
Subvert : To undermine the moral principles
Tardy : Late; slow in progress
Treachery : Violation of trust

COMPREHENSION QUESTIONS

I. Answer the following questions in about one or two words each.

1. Who was the king who fought for the liberation of Hindus?
2. What qualities make India a democratic country?
3. From where does Buddha borrow the rules of parliament?
4. What is the road to the salvation of the soul?
5. What are the principles of trinity?

II. Answer the following questions in about 50 words each.

1. What is the background of the speech?
2. What results in a good or bad constitution with reference to Ambedkar?
3. In what context, according to Ambedkar, did India lose the independence she had?
4. Explain the statement 'We must be determined to defend our independence with the last drop of our blood'.
5. What are the different thoughts that ran through the speaker's mind that made him anxious?

6. What are parliaments, and what is a parliamentary procedure according to the study made by Buddhist *Bhikshu Sanghas*?
7. Why is it quite possible to lose the democracy in a country like India?
8. What are Ambedkar's views on democracy?
9. 'These methods are nothing but the Grammar of Anarchy'. What are the methods that Ambedkar is referring to?
10. What was the warning that John Stuart Mill gave us for maintenance of democracy?
11. What is social democracy and political democracy?
12. What are the principles of life?
13. What is the principle that gives unity and solidarity to social life?
14. According to Ambedkar, what is the only way to serve the country?

III. Answer the following questions in about 200–250 words each.

1. Is the speaker optimistic or pessimistic in his tone? Give suitable example to substantiate your answer.
2. Give an account of the story of James Bryce told by Ambedkar to make us realize the sense of brotherhood?
3. Do you support the statement 'Without fraternity, equality and liberty will be no deeper than coats of paint'? Justify your answer with examples.
4. What are Ambedkar's reflections on the tasks that lie ahead of us?

IV. Use the following idioms in your own sentences. The first one is done for you.

Idiom : Have on the brain
Meaning : Thinking or talking about it all day long.
Example : He has just got engaged. Now, he has his fiance on his brain all the time.

1. Black sheep
2. Blow up in face
3. Cook someone's goose
4. Cry over spilt milk
5. Every cloud has a silver lining
6. Fish out of water

7. Live on the breadline
8. Sink your teeth into

V. Use the following phrasal verbs in your own sentences. The first one is done for you.

Phrasal verb : Keep on
Meaning : Continue doing something
Example : I told him to be quiet, but he *kept on* making noise.

1. Break up
2. Figure out
3. Hand out
4. Put through
5. Run into
6. Sign out
7. Think over
8. Wind up

VI. Writing skills

1. Write a speech on the Requirement of Changes in the Present Education System and present it before your class in the presence of your teacher.

VII. Speaking skills (speak for 3–4 minutes on the following topics)

1. Democracy in India
2. Necessary amendments considered in Indian constitution

Chapter Two

I have a Dream: An Independent, Developed and Strong India

Dr A.P.J. Abdul Kalam

Dr Avul Pakir Jainulabdeen Abdul Kalam was born on 15*th October* 1931 *in a Tamil Muslim family to Jainulabdeen, a boat owner at Rameswaram in Tamilnadu. He came from a poor background and started working at an early age to supplement his family income. Dr Kalam was the* 11*th president of India, during* 2002–2007. *This aerospace engineer was awarded the Bharat Ratna, the country's highest civilian honour in* 1997. *He is popularly known as missile man of India for his work.*

*Abdul Kalam is one of India's most distinguished scientists and is responsible for the development of India's first satellite launch vehicle SLV-*3. *Kalam authored* 15 *books on a variety of topics. His most significant works are Ignited Minds, Wings of Fire and India* 2020: *A Vision for a New Millennium. He is known for his inspiring speeches and fondness for the younger student community of the country.*

> Learning gives creativity, creativity leads to thinking, thinking provides knowledge, and knowledge makes you great.
>
> Dr A.P.J. Abdul Kalam

Dr Kalam delivered one of his best speeches at Indian Institute Technology of Hyderabad on 21st September 2013 that inspires the tender minds to unleash their power of mind and physical energy within India. He motivates the youngsters to transfigure the society in terms of technical, moral and economic development. His virtuous soul quests for India as a developed country, which indeed he wants to realize and make it true by changing the minds of youngsters toward a greater perspective and goal. His ethical soul strongly desires to see the youngsters and children as disciplined citizens who build up a strong and prosperous nation. The theme of his address is that he strongly condemns negativity of media. His speech is about developing conviction in ourselves and discarding the things that hold us back.

I have three visions for India. In 3000 years of our history, people from all over the world have come and invaded us, captured our lands, conquered our minds. From Alexander onward, the Greeks, the Turks, the Moguls, the Portuguese, the British, the French, the Dutch, all of them came and looted us, took over what was ours. Yet we have not done this to any other nation. We have not grabbed their land, their culture, their history. Why? Because we respect the freedom of others.

That is why my first vision is that of *freedom*. I believe that India got its first vision of this in 1857, when we started the War of Independence. It is this freedom that we must protect and nurture, and build on. If we are not free, no one will respect us.

My second vision for India's *development*: for 50 years we have been a developing nation. It is time we see ourselves as a developed nation. We are among the top five nations of the world in terms of GDP. We have 10% growth rate in most areas. Our poverty levels are falling. Our achievements are being globally recognized today. Yet, we lack the self-confidence to see ourselves as a developed nation, self-reliant.

I have a third vision: India must stand up to the world. Because I believe that unless India stands up to the world, no one will respect us. Only strength respects strength. We must be strong not only as a military power but also as an economic power. Both must go hand-in-hand. My good fortune was to have worked with three great minds Dr Vikram Sarabhai of the Department of Space, Professor Satish Dhawan, who succeeded him and Dr Brahm Prakash, father of nuclear material. I was lucky to have worked with all three of them closely and consider this a great opportunity of my life. I see four milestones in my career:

Twenty years I spent in ISRO. I was given the opportunity to be the project director for India's first satellite launch vehicle, SLV-3. The one that launched Rohini. These years played a very important role in my life as a scientist. After my ISRO years, I joined DRDO and got a chance to be part of India's guided missile program. It was my second bliss when Agni met its mission requirements in 1994.

The joy of participating with my team in these nuclear tests and proving to the world that India can make it – that we are no longer a developing nation, but one of them. It made me feel very proud as an Indian.

One day an orthopaedic surgeon from Nizam Institute of Medical Sciences visited my laboratory. He lifted the material and found it so light that he took me to his hospital and showed me his patients. There were these little girls and boys with heavy metallic calipers weighing over 3 kgs each, dragging their feet around.

He said to me: Please remove the pain of my patients. In three weeks, we made these Floor Reaction Orthosis 300 gram calipers and took them to the orthopaedic center. The children didn't believe their eyes. From dragging around a 3 kgs load on their legs, they could now move around! Their parents had tears in their eyes. That was my fourth bliss!

Why is the media here so negative? Why are we in India so embarrassed to recognize our own strengths, our achievements? We are such a great nation. We have so many amazing success stories, but we refuse to acknowledge them. Why?

We are the first in milk production.

We are number one in remote sensing satellites.

We are the second largest producer of wheat.

We are the second largest producer of rice.

Look at Dr Sudarshan, he has transferred the tribal village into a self-sustaining, self-driving unit.

There are millions of such achievements but our media is only obsessed with the bad news and failures and disasters.

I was in Tel Aviv once and I was reading the Israeli newspaper. It was the day after a lot of attacks and bombardments and deaths had taken place. The Hamas had struck. But the front page of the newspaper had the picture of a Jewish gentleman who in five years had transformed his desert land into an orchid and a granary.

It was this inspiring picture that everyone woke up to. The gory details of killings, bombardments, deaths, were inside in the newspaper, buried among other news. In India, we only read about death, sickness, terrorism, crime. Why are we so *negative*?

Another question: Why are we as a nation so obsessed with foreign things? We want foreign TVs, we want foreign shirts. We want foreign technology. Why this obsession with everything imported? Do we not realize that self-respect comes with self-reliance? I was in Hyderabad giving this lecture, when a 14-years-old girl asked me for my autograph. I asked her what her goal in life is. She replied: I want to live in a developed India. For her, you and I will have to build this developed India. You must proclaim. India is not an under-developed nation; it is a highly developed nation.

Do you have 10 minutes? Allow me to come back with vengeance. If yes, then read; otherwise, choice is yours.

You say that our government is inefficient.

You say that our laws are too old.

You say that the municipality does not pick up the garbage.

You say that the phones don't work, the railways are a joke, the airline is the worst in the world, mails never reach their destination.

You say that our country has been fed to the dogs and is the absolute pits.

You say, say.

In Singapore, you don't throw cigarette butts on the roads or eat in the stores. *You* are as proud of their underground links as they are. You pay $5 (approximately Rs. 60) to drive through Orchard Road (equivalent of Mahim Causeway or Pedder Road) between 5 PM and 8 PM. *You* come back to the parking lot to punch your parking ticket if you have overstayed in a restaurant or a shopping mall, irrespective of your status identity. In Singapore, you don't say anything, *do you? You* wouldn't dare to eat in public during Ramadan, in Dubai. *You* would not dare to go out without your head covered in Jeddah. *You* would not dare to buy an employee of the telephone exchange in London at 10 pounds (Rs. 650) a month to, 'see to it that my STD and ISD calls are billed to someone else'.

You would not dare to speed beyond 55 mph (88 km/h) in Washington, and then tell the traffic cop, '*Jaanta hai sala main kaun hoon?* (Do you know who I am?) I am so and so's son. Take your two bucks and get lost'. *You* wouldn't chuck an empty coconut shell anywhere other than the garbage pail on the beaches in Australia and New Zealand. Why don't *you* spit *paan* on the streets of Tokyo? Why don't *you* use examination jockeys or buy fake certificates in Boston? We are still talking of the same *you*. *You* who can respect and conform to a foreign system in other countries but cannot in your own. You who will throw papers and cigarettes on the road the moment you touch Indian ground. If you can be an involved and appreciative citizen in an alien country, why cannot you be the same here in India?

Once in an interview, the famous ex-municipal commissioner of Bombay, Mr Tinaikar, had a point to make. 'Rich people's dogs are walked on the streets to leave their affluent droppings all over the place', he said. And then the same people turn around to criticize and blame the authorities for inefficiency and dirty pavements. What do they expect the officers to do? Go down with broom every time their dog feels the pressure in his bowels? In America, every dog owner has to clean up after his pet has done the job. Same in Japan. 'Will the Indian citizen do that here?' He's right. We go to the polls to choose. We sit back wanting to be pampered and expect the government to do everything for us whilst our contribution is totally negative. We expect the government to clean up, but we are not going to stop chucking garbage all over the place, nor are we going to stop to pick up a stray piece of paper and throw it in the bin. We expect the railways to provide clean bathrooms, but we are not going to learn the proper use of bathrooms.

We want Indian Airlines and Air India to provide the best of food and toiletries, but we are not going to stop pilfering at the least opportunity. This applies even to the staff who is known not to pass on the service to the public. When it comes to burning social issues such as those related to women, dowry, girl child and others, we make loud drawing room protestations and continue to do the reverse at home. Our excuse? 'It's the whole system which has to change, how will it matter if I alone forego my sons' rights to a dowry'.

So who's going to change the system? What does a system consist of? Very conveniently for us, it consists of our neighbours, other households, other cities, other communities and the government. But definitely not me and *you*. When it comes to us actually making a positive contribution to the system, we lock ourselves along with our families into a safe cocoon and look into the distance at countries far away and wait for a Mr Clean to come along and work miracles for us with a majestic sweep of his hand or we leave the country and run away. Like lazy cowards hounded by our fears, we run to America to bask in their glory and praise their system. When New York becomes insecure, we run to England. When England experiences unemployment, we take the next flight out to the Gulf. When the Gulf is war struck, we demand to be rescued and brought home by the Indian government.

Everybody is out to abuse and rape the country. Nobody thinks of feeding the system. Our conscience is mortgaged to money.

I am echoing J.F. Kennedy's words to his fellow Americans to relate to Indians:

'Ask what we can do for India and do what has to be done to make India what America and other western countries are today'.

Let's do what India needs from us.

GLOSSARY

Acknowledge	: Accept the truth of, confirm receipt of
Affluent	: Somebody who is wealthy
Bombardment	: Attack with bombs or other missiles
Caliper	: A metal support for a person's leg
Milestone	: An important event in a person's life or career
Pampered	: Treat very indulgently
Vengeance	: Desire for revenge

COMPREHENSION QUESTIONS

I. Answer the following questions in about one or two words each.

1. What do we expect the government to do?
2. What does the system consist of?
3. Which facility do we expect railways to provide?
4. Why wouldn't people dare to eat in public during Ramadan in Dubai?
5. What is it that we are so embarrassed to recognize?

II. Answer the following questions in about 100 words each.

1. Why is the media here so negative? Substantiate views.
2. Briefly describe A.P.J. Abdul Kalam's vision.
3. What was the bliss he bought to little girls and boys with heavy metallic calipers?

III. Answer the following questions in about 150 words each.

1. Write about the changes Abdul Kalam would like to see in Indians in terms of discipline compared with foreign countries.
2. Summarize Abdul Kalam speech in your own words.

III. Match the following idioms with their meanings given in column B.

Column A		Column B
1. Cut both ways	:	To try very hard
2. Come off with flying colours	:	An obstacle
3. Like a fish out of water	:	To have advantages as well as disadvantages

4. Gain ground : To become more popular or accepted
5. Move heaven and earth : Uncomfortable among people who are different from you
6. A stumbling block : To be successful
7. Face the music : A rogue, disreputable member
8. A black sheep : To accept blame or punishment for something wrong you have done

IV. Fill in the blanks by choosing the appropriate phrasal verb from the list given in the parenthesis.

(admitted of, lookup, ran out of, let down, backed up)

1. He ________________the manager's proposal.
2. The statue ____________only a single interpretation.
3. I will take time to_______________words in dictionary.
4. I felt__________ when India lost the match.
5. The bike did not start as it ____________petrol.

Chapter Three

Nobel Lecture

Kailash Satyarthi

Kailash Satyarthi is an Indian children's rights advocate and an activist. He is a Gandhian at heart. He founded the Bachpan Bachao Andolan in 1980. *His work is recognized through various national and international honours and awards, including the Nobel Peace Prize of* 2014. *Kailash Satyarthi has saved tens of thousands of lives. He gave up a promising career as an electrical engineer and dedicated his life to helping millions of children in India who are forced into slavery by powerful and corrupt business – and land owners. His original idea was daring and dangerous. He decided to mount raids on factories – factories frequently manned by armed guards where children and often entire families were held captive as bonded workers.*

In this speech in Oslo on 10*th December* 2014*, he talks about the liberation of child labour. He represents the sounds of silence, the cry of innocence, and the face of invisibility. He talks about the dreams of the underprivileged children. He says there's no greater violence than to deny the dreams of our children. His only aim is to make every child free to grow and develop, to eat and sleep well, to be able to go to school and also to dream. He says that our biggest crisis knocking on the doors of humanity is intolerance.*

Let Us Globalize Compassion, and Set Our Children Free

With a warm heart, I recall how thousands of times I have been liberated each time I have freed a child from slavery. In the first smile of freedom on their beautiful faces, I see the Gods smiling.

I give the biggest credit of this honour to my movement's Kaalu Kumar, Dhoom Das and Adarsh Kishore from India and Iqbal Masih from Pakistan who made the supreme sacrifice for protecting the freedom and dignity of children.

My journey from the great land of Lord Buddha, Guru Nanak and Mahatma Gandhi, India to Norway is a connect between the two centres of global peace and brotherhood, ancient and modern. I represent here the sound of silence, the cry of innocence and, the face of invisibility. I have come here to share the voices and dreams of our children – *our children*, because they are all our children.

I have looked into their frightened and exhausted eyes. And I have heard their urgent questions: twenty years ago, in the foothills of the Himalayas, I met a small, skinny boy. He asked me, 'Is the world so poor that it cannot give me a toy and a book, instead of forcing me to take a tool or gun?' I met with a Sudanese child-soldier who was kidnapped by an extremist militia. As his first training, he was forced to kill his friends and family. He asked me, 'What is my fault?' Twelve years ago, a child-mother from the streets of Colombia – trafficked, raped, enslaved – asked me this, 'I have never had a dream. Can my child have one?'

There is no greater violence than to deny the dreams of our children.

The single aim of my life is that every child is:

free to be a child,
free to grow and develop,
free to eat, sleep, see daylight,
free to laugh and cry,
free to play,
free to learn, free to go to school, and above all,
free to dream.

All the great religions tell us to care for children. Jesus said: 'Let the children come to me; do not hinder them, for the kingdom of God belongs to them'. The Holy Quran says, 'Kill not your children because of poverty'. I refuse to accept that all the temples and mosques and churches and prayer houses have no place for the dreams of our children. I refuse to accept that the world is so poor, when just one week of global spending on armies is enough to bring all of our children into classrooms.

I refuse to accept that all the laws and constitutions, and the judges and the police are not able to protect our children.

I refuse to accept that the shackles of slavery can ever be stronger than the quest for freedom.

I refuse to accept.

I am privileged to work with many courageous souls who also refuse to accept. We have never given up against any threat and attack, and we will never. Undoubtedly, progress has been made in the last couple of decades. The number of out of school children has been halved. Child mortality and malnutrition has been reduced, and millions of child deaths have been prevented. The number of child labourers in the world has been reduced by a third. Make no mistake, great challenges still remain.

Friends, the biggest crisis knocking on the doors of humanity today is intolerance.

We have utterly failed in imparting education to our children – an education that gives the meaning and objective of life and a secure future, an education that builds a sense of global citizenship among the young people. I am afraid that the day is not far when the cumulative result of this failure will culminate in unprecedented violence that will be suicidal for humankind.

Yet, young people like Malala, are rising up everywhere and choosing peace over violence, tolerance over extremism and courage over fear.

Solutions are not found only in the deliberations in conferences and prescriptions from a distance. They lie in small groups and local organizations and individuals, who confront the problem every day, even if they remain unrecognized and unknown to the world.

Eighteen years ago, millions of my brothers and sisters in 103 countries marched across 80,000 km. And, a new international law against child labour was born. We have done this.

You may ask, what can one person do? Let me tell you a story I remember from my childhood: A terrible fire had broken out in the forest. All the animals were running away, including the lion, king of the forest. Suddenly, the lion saw a tiny bird rushing toward the fire. He asked the bird, 'what are you doing?' To the lion's surprise, the bird replied, 'I am on my way to extinguish the fire'. He laughed and said, 'how can you kill the fire with just one drop of water, in your beak?' The bird was adamant, and said, 'But I am doing my bit'.

You and I live in the age of rapid globalization. We are connected through high-speed Internet. We exchange goods and services in a single global market. Each day, thousands of flights connect us to every corner of the globe.

But there is one serious disconnect. It is the lack of compassion. Let us inculcate and transform the individuals' compassion into a global movement. Let us globalize compassion. Not passive compassion, but transformative compassion that leads to justice, equality and freedom.

Mahatma Gandhi said, 'If we are to teach real peace in this world …, we shall have to begin with the children'. I humbly add, let us unite the world through the compassion for our children.

Whose children are they who stitch footballs, yet have never played with one? They are our children. Whose children are they who mine stones and minerals? They are our children. Whose children are they who harvest cocoa, yet do not know the taste of a chocolate? They are all our children.

Devli was born into intergenerational debt and bonded labour in India. Sitting in my car immediately after her rescue, the 8-year-old girl asked, 'Why did you not come earlier?' Her angry question still shakes me, and has the power to shake the world. Her question is for all of us. Why did we not come earlier? What are we waiting for? How many more Devlis will we allow to go without rescue? How many more girls will be abducted, confined and abused? Children, like Devli, across the world are questioning our inaction and watching our actions.

We need collective actions with a sense of urgency. Every single minute matters, every single child matters, every single childhood matters.

I challenge the passivity and pessimism surrounding our children. I challenge this culture of silence, this culture of neutrality.

I, therefore, call upon all the governments, intergovernmental agencies, businesses, faith leaders, the civil society and each one of us to put an end to all forms of violence against children. Slavery, trafficking, child marriages, child labour, sexual abuse and illiteracy have no place in any civilized society.

Friends, we can do this.

Governments must make child-friendly policies and invest in education and young people.

Businesses must be more responsible and open to innovative partnerships.

Intergovernmental agencies must work together to accelerate action.

Global civil society must rise above business-as-usual and scattered agendas.

Faith leaders and institutions, and all of us must stand with our children.

We must be bold, we must be ambitious and we must have the will. We must keep our promises.

Over 50 years ago, on the first day of my school, I met a cobbler boy my age sitting at the school gate, polishing shoes. I asked my teachers these questions: 'Why is he working outside? Why is he not coming to school with me?' My teachers had no answer. One day, I gathered the courage to ask the boy's father. He said, 'Sir, I have never thought about it. We are just born to work'. This made me angry. It still makes me angry. I challenged it then, and I am challenging it today.

As a child, I had a vision of tomorrow. That cobbler boy was studying with me in my classroom. Now, that tomorrow has become *today*. I am *today*, and you are *today*. *Today*, it is time for every child to have the right to life, the right to freedom, the right to health, the right to education, the right to safety, the right to dignity, the right to equality and the right to peace.

Today, beyond the darkness, I see the smiling faces of our children in the blinking stars. *Today*, in every wave of every ocean, I see our children playing and dancing. *Today*, in every plant, tree and mountain, I see that little cobbler boy sitting with me in the classroom.

I want you to see and feel this *today* inside you. My dear sisters and brothers, may I ask you to close your eyes and put your hand close to your heart for a moment? Can you feel the child inside you? Now, listen to this child. I am sure you can!

Today, I see thousands of Mahatma Gandhis, Martin Luther Kings and Nelson Mandelas marching forward and calling on us. The boys and girls have joined. I have joined in. We ask you to join too.

Let us democratize knowledge.

Let us universalize justice.

Together, let us globalize compassion, for our children!

I call upon you in this room, and all across the world.

I call for a march from exploitation to education, from poverty to shared prosperity, a march from slavery to liberty, and a march from violence to peace. Let us march from darkness to light. Let us march from mortality to divinity.

GLOSSARY

Abduct	:	Illegally take away by force or deception
Child mortality	:	The death of infants under the age of five
Compassion	:	Understanding, sympathy
Culminate	:	Conclude
Deliberation	:	Consideration, pondering
Enslaved	:	Make somebody a slave
Extremist militia	:	Revolutionary band of soldier
Hinder	:	Obstruct
Inculcate	:	Teach and impress by frequent repetitions
Malnutrition	:	Starvation
Neutrality	:	Non-participation in a dispute or war or absence of strong feeling
Passivity	:	Remaining inactive
Quest	:	Pursuit
Rescue	:	Recovery, reclamation
Shackles	:	Restraints
Unprecedented	:	Unique/Extraordinary

COMPREHENSION QUESTIONS

I. Answer the following questions in about one or two words each.

1. When did Satyarthi make this speech?
2. Whose dreams does Satyarthi talk about?
3. What is the biggest crisis knocking on the doors of humanity today?
4. According to Satyarthi, what can give us a secure future?
5. What do the great religions say?

II. Answer the following questions in about 100 words each.

1. According to Satyarthi, how can bonded labour be eradicated?
2. Where according to Satyarthi can one find 'solutions'?
3. What do we understand from his example where he talks about a bird trying to extinguish the fire in the forest?
4. Why do you think he refuses to accept that the world is poor?

III. Answer the following questions in about 200 words each.

1. What is the 'dream' that Satyarthi talks about in the speech?
2. What are the suggestions made by the speaker in order to achieve our 'dreams'?
3. What according to the speaker could be done to achieve the dreams of the underprivileged children?
4. 'As a child, I had a vision for tomorrow'. How does Satyarthi support his statement?

IV. Use the following idioms in your own sentences. The first one is done for you.

Idiom : Herding cats
Meaning : Involving coordination of many different groups
Example : I try to get two parties together, and it is like *herding cats.*

1. A hard nut to crack
2. At the nick of the moment
3. Break the ice
4. Lend an ear
5. Pack of lies
6. To leave no stone unturned
7. Up in arms

V. Complete the sentences by choosing the appropriate phrasal verbs from the following options.

1. If you want to stay at this school, you must _______the rules.
   (a) abide by
   (b) comply
   (c) follow up

2. Don't forget the date. I'm ________your help.
   (a) trust
   (b) believe up
   (c) banking on

3. I told her a joke to try and ________.
   (a) laugh with her
   (b) cheer her
   (c) cheer her up

4. She __________at school and had to study harder.
   (a) fell behind
   (b) fell upon
   (c) fell into

5. He promised to ________the money he borrowed.
   (a) give back
   (b) give into
   (c) give up

Chapter Four

Life is Not Milk and Roses

C.V. Raman

C.V. Raman – the man, the scientist, the legacy:
Look at the resplendent colours on the soap bubbles!
Why is the sea blue?
What makes diamond glitter?
What makes Hubli so special?
*Ask the right questions, and nature will open the doors to her secrets.**

One of the most prominent Indian scientists in history, C.V. Raman (Chandra Sekhara Venkata Raman) was the first Indian to win the Nobel Prize in science. He received it for his illustrious 1930 *discovery, now commonly known as the 'Raman Effect'. It is immensely surprising that Raman used an equipment worth merely Rs.* 200 *to make this discovery. The Raman Effect is now examined with the help of equipment worth almost millions of rupees. Sir C.V. Raman became the Fellow of the Royal Society of London in* 1924*. His sincere advice to aspiring scientists was that* 'Scientific research needed independent thinking and hard work, not equipment'.

Sir C.V. Raman's convocation address delivered at Agra University on 18 *November* 1950 *unleashes the philosophy of human life and rejuvenates the souls of youngsters by reviving their dormant inner energies. The speech excavates the ensconced sources that are in abundance and pleads to the youth to utilize them. It proclaims the greatness of indomitable spirit that invokes the young minds,*

*Parameswaran, Uma. C.V. Raman: A Biography. India: Penguin, 2011

motivating them to the rightful path. His glaring lines spread the radiance of knowledge and inspiration. His emotional words hold a mirror to the modern society. He portrays that life is not a bed of roses but a bed of thorns, and the phenomenon of life lies not in luxury but in simplicity. He urges the youth to venerate and adore nature, and concurrently render due respect to science.

His speech underlies the philosophy that we come with nothing and go with nothing, but until we survive on this planet, something illuminating is to be done. As nature sustains us, we too have to sustain it. Raman finds glory in giving but not in expecting. He says that Nature and experience are the best teachers that lustre our lives. As nature renders selfless service, we too should render altruistic service. He emphasizes that man must be the creator, but he should not be the destroyer. He observes the fact that 'Service to nature is service to God'. And finally, he says that with perseverant endeavour and docile and meek demeanour, one can reach the pinnacle of success and can raise from the nadir to the zenith.

His stupendous extempore reflects his spontaneity and shows that he is a repository of knowledge.

It is no small honour to be asked to address the Convocation of a University in India, and certainly it is a unique experience for me, at any rate, to be called upon to address a University Convocation at one place a second time.

I know poverty and misery, and I quite appreciate by personal experience what it is to be poor, what it is to have no clothes, what it is to have no books, what it is to struggle through life, what it is to walk through the streets without an umbrella, without conveyance along miles in dusty wards – I have been through it all and I can understand the difficulties that most of you graduates have to face up today. I'm speaking from a long experience of 60 years. Please do not imagine that all the 60 years are milk and roses. To be able to accomplish something I want to tell you that you have to go through such experience.

I admit, success in life is not always to the intelligent or the strong and it is to some extent a bit of a gamble, but nonetheless those who have got their minds right and those who know their job will sooner or later – sooner perhaps than later – make their way in life. But they should not be disappointed if they do not. They have to face up to life and take it as they find it. This is the kind of philosophy that I have learnt by experience, and I make a free gift of it to you all.

What I say is this that the great things in life are not really great things in life. The Nobel Prize, the FRS and the like, many of them leave a bitter taste in the mouth. What I love is to enjoy the common things of life. I am happy that I am still able to sleep at night, provided I have three miles walk in the evening. I am still able to enjoy a good lunch or a good dinner. I am still able to look at the blue sky and like it. I still like to walk in the open fields and like the smell of the ragi or the jowar. I feel a younger man when I see the Babul flower and say, God has given us these wonderful things. That is the real philosophy of life – to appreciate what we see around us.

We think that happiness consists in going to pictures and seeing thrilling films and techni-colour dramas. Not at all! The great things in life are the God-given things which cost nothing. What you need is the desire to appreciate them. If you have your minds and hearts open, you have around you things which give you joy. There is the butterfly jumping about in flourishing colours on all sides. Look at this wonderful thing that God has given for our enjoyment.

We have to love nature and appreciate nature and appreciate her wonderful gifts, her marvellous ingenuity, her resourcefulness, her infinite variety. It is the same thing that has inspired me all my life. I study science not because anything is going to happen to me, but because I feel it is a kind of worship of this great Goddess, Nature, of which we are a part. That has been my inspiration as a man of science. I feel now that is one thing that can always make a man happy, the small things in life not only in nature – our old friends, old music and the things that we have around us. Many a time, I would like to go back to them.

It may be a sign of cynicism, but I would like to go back to the common things of life. A glass of cold water, for example, gives us vigour and freshness (*Dr Raman, in so saying, drank from a glass of cold water amidst laughter*). I can assure you there is no pleasure in this world for a healthy man, than after a vigorous exercise or doing something hard just to go home and have a glass of cold water. If you have lost the capacity to appreciate that, you may as well drink a cup of hemlock, as Socrates had to do.

I have another word to say. We all speak of patriotism. What is patriotism? I want you to think it over and in the last analysis bring down patriotism to a physical term. I have thought over the problem. Patriotism as well as a number of things boil down to the love of the earth. We are of the earth. When we die we return to the earth, dust to dust, ashes to ashes; the human body whether cremated or buried returns to earth. Seeta was of earth and returned to earth. This good earth sustains us. On earth grows green grass, which the cow eats and which a vegetarian like myself as well as a non-vegetarian gets milk from. Ultimately, it is the earth and the things that grow upon it that sustain us and feed us and make human life possible. I think ultimately the love for the land means the love of the earth which has borne us and which sustains us. I want you to appreciate the meaning of love of earth.

The love of mother earth should be shown by tending her. If she is ruthlessly raped and destroyed, we shall also die with her. The tremendous problem of lack of food in the country boils down to this that we have left the love of earth to ignorant people who know nothing of the advance of science. We, educated people who understand science, do not love mother earth. Knowledge of science will make us create anything, but unless we have that vision, that desire to love mother earth, we shall not make any advance.

I think it is a duty laid on every educated man to create something, to see something grow. I say this not as a part of the 'grow more food campaign', I have not been paid to do propaganda for it. I am telling you about it in the same spirit that a famous Roman did. When once Rome was in danger the people wanted to have him as a dictator to save Rome. When they went to him they found him ploughing the land with his own hands and tending his farm. After he became a dictator, he went back to the land and said, these plants I have grown, I give them water, I give them labour and they repay. We should work in this spirit.

The more you help a man, the less grateful he is to you. It is, however, our duty to help fellow beings, and we should not expect them to show any gratitude in return. If they do show, we are very happy and more fortunate. The plant on earth will never fail to repay any attention that we bestow on it. We must go back to earth and regard it as our supreme duty to do something to produce the things on which we live.

It is a great privilege to see such a great body of young people, women and men alike who are entering the pathways of life after a course of study in colleges and university, and to be allowed to speak to them and making a heart to heart speech gives me great pleasure.

I never believe in manuscript eloquence or in after-dinner speeches carefully prepared 24 hours beforehand. I always believe in standing up in front of my audience, appreciate the situation and speak to them heart to heart. I have no desire at all to inflict unwanted advice on you. I want you to think over what I have told you and see if some little thing that I have said may prove the seed of some great achievement on your part, sustain you, encourage you, elevate your hearts above and so push you on in life that you may rise triumphant over all the difficulties and all the troubles that are the common lot of the common man in India today.*

GLOSSARY

Babul flower	: Acacia, popularly known as Babul, is a large tree, up to darkish grey bark and yellow flowers in spherical heads
Convocation	: A large formal meeting especially of church officials or members of a university
Conveyance	: The process of taking somebody or something from one place to another
Cynicism	: An inclination to believe that people are motivated purely by self-interest; scepticism
Dusty wards	: Dusty paths; paths covered with dust or narrow ways
FRS	: The Fellowship of Royal Society of London; Raman is the only Indian FRS who resigned from the Fellowship of the Society
Gamble	: To risk losing something in the hope of being successful
Inflict	: Impose something unwelcome on
Milk and roses	: Full of comforts

*India Visit Information. "Indian Personalities - Chandrasekhara Venkata Raman." Last accessed August 11, 2015. http://www.indiavisitinformation.com/indian-personality/Chandrasekhara-Venkata.shtml

Patriotism : Love of your country and have the willingness to defend it

Socrates : Socrates was a classical Greek philosopher credited as one of the founders of Western philosophy. He is an enigmatic figure known chiefly through the accounts of classical writers

Tend : To be likely to do something or to happen in a particular way because this is what often or usually happens

Vigour : Physical strength and good health

COMPREHENSION QUESTIONS

I. Answer the following questions in about one or two words each.

1. Expand FRS.
2. What are ragi and jowar?
3. What is meant by techni-colour dramas?
4. Write the definition of cynicism?

II. Answer the following questions in about 100 words each.

1. What does the speaker appreciate by personal experience and what kind of philosophy has he learnt? Elaborate your answer.
2. Explain Raman's simplicity of life.
3. What has inspired Raman all his life and what are the things he speaks about?

III. Answer the following questions in about 200 words each.

1. Summarize the inspiring philosophy of life as elaborated by Sir C.V. Raman.
2. 'The more you help a man, the less grateful he is to you'. Elaborate and justify this in terms of Sir C.V. Raman.

IV. Use the following phrasal verbs in sentences of your own. The first one is done for you.

Phrasal verb : Face up
Meaning : To accept that a difficult situation exists
Example : You have to *face up* to many challenges in your life.

Phrasal verb : Go through
Meaning : Undergo, experience

Phrasal verb : Think over
Meaning : To consider an idea or plan carefully before making a decision

Phrasal verb : Bring down
Meaning : To reduce the amount or level of something

Phrasal verb : Boil down to
Meaning : Amount to; be essentially a matter of

Phrasal verb : Lay on
Meaning : To tell or show something to someone, especially when you do not expect them to like it

V. Match the following idioms in column A with their meanings in column B.

	Column A		Column B
1.	Upset the apple cart	:	A cause of argument
2.	Alpha and Omega	:	To find something out sbut not wish to reveal the source of information
3.	Get the axe	:	A marriage or relationship between young person and a much older person
4.	A case of May and December	:	To spoil plans, or to obstruct progress
5.	A little bird told me	:	The beginning and the end
6.	A bolt from the blue	:	Taking a risk which may end up in the situation going wrong or right
7.	A bone of contention	:	To be dismissed from a post
8.	A bit of a gamble	:	A sudden, unexpected happening

Chapter Five

Stay Hungry, Stay Foolish

Steve Jobs

Steve Jobs, a quiet yet effective CEO, is known for completely changing the landscape of the computer industry. He was widely recognized as a charismatic and design-driven pioneer of the personal computer revolution and for his influential career in the computer and consumer electronics fields, transforming 'one industry after another, from computers and smart phones to music and movies'.

Jobs received a number of honours and public recognition for his influence in the technology and music industries. He has been referred to as 'legendary', *a* 'futurist' *and a* 'visionary', *and has been described as the* 'father of the digital revolution', *a* 'master of innovation', 'the master evangelist of the digital age' *and a* 'design perfectionist'.

The following text is an excerpt from Steve Jobs famous commencement speech to graduating class of Stanford University in 2005. *Finding a career based on students' passions was the central theme of the speech. In his speech, he expressed the importance of being true to oneself and living authentically throughout one's career. He talked about dropping out of college, being fired from Apple and being diagnosed with cancer. His speech epitomized his personal brand. It has been described as* 'life-changing' *and* '*career transforming*'.

I am honoured to be with you today at your commencement from one of the finest universities in the world. I never graduated from college. Truth be told, this is the closest I've ever gotten to a college graduation.

Today, I want to tell you three stories from my life. That's it. No big deal. Just three stories.

The First Story is about Connecting the Dots

I dropped out of Reed College after the first 6 months, but then stayed around as a drop-in for another 18 months or so before I really quit. So why did I drop out? After 6 months, I couldn't see the value in it. I had no idea what I wanted to do with my life and no idea how college was going to help me figure it out. And here I was spending all of the money my parents had saved their entire life. So I decided to drop out and trust that it would all work out OK. The minute I dropped out, I could stop taking the required classes that didn't interest me, and begin dropping in on the ones that looked interesting.

It wasn't all romantic. I didn't have a dorm room, so I slept on the floor in friends' rooms, I returned coke bottles for the 5¢ deposits to buy food with, and I would walk the 7 miles across town every Sunday night to get one good meal a week at the Hare Krishna temple. I loved it. And much of what I stumbled into by following my curiosity and intuition turned out to be priceless later on. Again, you can't connect the dots looking forward; you can only connect them looking backwards. So you have to trust that the dots will somehow connect in your future. You have to trust in something – your gut, destiny, life, karma, whatever. This approach has never let me down, and it has made all the difference in my life.

My Second Story is about Love and Loss

I was lucky – I found what I loved to do early in life. Woz and I started Apple in my parents' garage when I was 20. We worked hard, and in 10 years Apple had grown from just the two of us in a garage into a $2-billion company with over 4000 employees. We had just released our finest creation – the Macintosh – a year earlier, and I had just turned 30. And then I got fired.

How can you get fired from a company you started? Well, as Apple grew, we hired someone who I thought was very talented to run the company with me, and for the first year or so things went well. But then our visions of the future began to diverge and eventually we had a falling out. When we did, our Board of Directors sided with him. So at 30, I was out. And very publicly out.

What had been the focus of my entire adult life was gone, and it was devastating. I didn't see it then, but it turned out that getting fired from Apple was the best thing that could have ever happened to me. The heaviness of being successful was replaced by the lightness of being a beginner again, less sure about everything. It freed me to enter one of the most creative periods of my life.

During the next 5 years, I started a company named NeXT, another company named Pixar and fell in love with an amazing woman who would become my wife.

Pixar went on to create the world's first computer-animated feature film, Toy Story, and is now the most successful animation studio in the world. In a remarkable turn of events, Apple bought NeXT, I returned to Apple, and the technology we developed at NeXT is at the heart of Apple's current renaissance. I'm pretty sure none of this would have happened if I hadn't been fired from Apple. It was awful tasting medicine, but I guess the patient needed it. Sometimes life hits you in the head with a brick. Don't lose faith. I'm convinced that the only thing that kept me going was that I loved what I did. You've got to find what you love.

And that is as true for your work as it is for your lovers. Your work is going to fill a large part of your life, and the only way to be truly satisfied is to do what you believe is great work. And the only way to do great work is to love what you do. If you haven't found it yet, keep looking. Don't settle. As with all matters of the heart, you'll know when you find it. And, like any great relationship, it just gets better and better as the years roll on.

My Third Story is about Death

About a year ago, I was diagnosed with cancer. My doctor advised me to go home and get my affairs in order, which is doctor's code for prepare to die. It means to try to tell your kids everything you thought you'd have the next 10 years to tell them in just a few months. This was the closest I've been to facing death, and I hope it's the closest I get for a few more decades.

When I was young, there was an amazing publication called The Whole Earth Catalog – created by a fellow named Stewart Brand – which was one of the bibles of my generation. Stewart and his team put out several issues of *The Whole Earth Catalog*, and then when it had run its course, they put out a final issue. It was the mid-1970s, and I was your age. On the back cover of their final issue was a photograph of an early morning country road, the kind you might find yourself hitch-hiking on if you were so adventurous.

Beneath it were the words: 'Stay Hungry. Stay Foolish'. It was their farewell message as they signed off. Stay Hungry. Stay Foolish. And I have always wished that for myself. And now, as you graduate to begin anew, I wish that for you. Stay Hungry. Stay Foolish.

GLOSSARY

5¢	:	5 cents
Diagnose	:	Identify the nature of the medical condition
Dorm	:	A dormitory, (North American) a university or college hall of residence, or hostel
Drop-in	:	(*Noun*) One who casually drops in (*Adjective*) Visited on an informal basis without booking or appointments
Excerpt	:	A short extract from a film, broadcast, or piece of music or writing
Figure it out	:	Discover, determine
Got fired	:	Got dismissed from a job
Gut (in the plural)	:	Ability and will to face up to adversity or unpleasantness
Hitch-hiking	:	Travel by getting free lifts in passing vehicles
Intuition	:	The ability to understand something instinctively, without the need for conscious reasoning
Renaissance	:	A revival of or renewed interest in something
Stumble	:	Trip or momentarily lose one's balance; almost fall

COMPREHENSION QUESTIONS

I. Answer the following questions in about one or two words each.

1. What did Steve Jobs do to get food and a good meal?
2. According to Steve Jobs, how can you connect the dots?
3. Who started Apple?
4. What were the companies started by Steve Jobs after getting fired from Apple?

II. Answer the following questions in about 100 words each.

1. Illustrate the first story of Steve Jobs.
2. Illustrate the second story of Steve Jobs.
3. Illustrate the third story of Steve Jobs.

III. Answer the following questions in about 200 words each.

1. Do you support Steve Jobs' stories about his life? How do you justify your answer?
2. 'Stay Hungry. Stay Foolish'. Justify the statement in terms of Steve Jobs.

IV. Use the following idioms in your own sentences. The first one is done for you.

Idiom : Once in a blue moon
Meaning : Very rarely
Example : Mokshitha goes to college *once in a blue moon.*

1. Beat about the bush
2. Black and blue
3. Black sheep
4. Eleventh hour
5. Fish out of the water
6. Meet both ends
7. Naked eye
8. Nip in the bud

V. Use the following phrasal verbs in your own sentences. The first one is done for you.

Phrasal verb : Let down
Meaning : Disappoint
Example : You promised to come to the party, so don't *let* me *down*!

1. Egg on
2. Figure out
3. Get off
4. Hand back
5. Move out
6. Pass away
7. Play up
8. Wear out

Short Stories

Chapter Six

Death of a Hero

Jai Nimbkar

Jai Nimbkar is one of the Indian writers who has made a mark of her own. Her stories talk about the sufferings undergone by the sensitive persons in a world of uncertain values of the society. Her characters depict the lives of ordinary people from lower middle class and labour class whom we often encounter on the streets. She has been writing in Marathi and has published two novels and a collection of sketches of women. Her popular novels are Come Rain (1993), A Joint Venture (1988) *and* Temporary Answers (1974).

The story is about a man with integrity Mr Tagde, a school teacher (about to retire in 3 years). The story is about his fight against injustice. As we keep reading on, we realize that there is a transformation that takes place in his personality: a transformation from a timid teacher into a real hero who puts his career and life at risk. However, we notice that his sacrifice goes to waste as he is forced to compromise at the end by taking away the need for this heroic sacrifice.

'Sit down', the principal said. But Mr Tagde continued to stand, gaining courage from his own straight-backed stance, because he was beginning to feel a little afraid now.

The principal looked unhappy. He disliked being forced to perform this sort of an unpleasant task.

'I wish you would consider withdrawing this report', he said.

'I am sorry sir, I cannot do that', Mr Tagde said. He was pleased with his unwavering voice and uncompromising words.

'It will be a very damaging report if put on record'.

'It is a factual report on very damaging conduct'.

'You are asking for the boy's expulsion from school. Don't you think the punishment is too harsh for a few boyish pranks?'

'He has spoiled benches in my classroom by scoring them with a razor blade. He has made the blackboard useless by scratching on it with a piece of tin. He has broken several window panes by throwing stones at them. Yesterday he broke another one and the flying pieces of glass hurt a pupil badly. That is not all. Many girl students have complained by having their books, notebooks and pens stolen, and I could get evidence that the More boy is behind it. Also there have been complaints from girls that he stops them on street and shouts obscenities at them and threatens to beat them up. The report contains all this and more. I cannot agree with you that the behaviour can be called merely boyish pranks'.

The principal spread his hands in a helpless gesture. He looked at Mr Tagde, a small thin man in his slightly yellowed dhoti and his coat of a nondescript colour and his black cap. Outwardly he looked the same as he had for the last 15 years that the principal had known him: a solid teacher, a mature and rational man, suitably diplomatic in his dealings with those in authority, a good man to work with.

The principal, heartened by his scrutiny of his colleague, continued more hopefully.

'But the boy has already been punished for this misconduct', he said. 'Why rake it all up again?'

'When More hurt that boy yesterday – the glass cut his cheek, and small pieces of it had to be removed from the wound at the government dispensary – I decided that he had to be stopped before he did any further damage. The boy who was hurt comes from a poor family. His parents are not in a position to do anything about More'.

'I am sure Veerendra did not mean this particular boy any harm'.

'Most certainly he did not. He merely wanted to break a windowpane and disrupt my class. If in the process someone got hurt that was an added bonus'.

Mr Tagde surprised himself at the sudden intensity of his anger. The kind of anger he had felt when he saw the irregular star of the broken window and the blood running down the boy's cheek, and anger which sends the blood rushing to one's eyes and momentarily blurs one's vision and one's fear.

'There is no call to be sarcastic, Mr Tagde', the principal said sharply. 'I am not condoning the boy's behaviour. I am merely suggesting that you are putting too serious a construction on it'.

Mr Tagde neither moved nor spoke.

'I could refuse to put the matter on the agenda for the school committee meeting, you know?'

'In that case I shall be forced to send a copy of the report to each committee member and one to *Vartavihar*. I am sure the editor would find it interesting enough to publish in the next edition'.

This was an extempore thought, and his elation at having stumbled on it gave Mr Tagde more confidence. The principal made a feeble attempt at laughing. 'Come now, you don't mean that', he said.

'You are aware', the principal said, carefully enunciating each word as though to make sure Mr Tagde heard it, 'that the chairman of the school committee is Veerendra's uncle?'

'I am'.

'You still want this report to go up to their committee?'

'All right, I shall forward it as your personal recommendation, for consideration at the meeting to be held on Friday evening'.

That's right, save your own skin; don't endorse it, Mr Tagde thought, looking with distaste at the principal's bland face. Then he thought, I have no right to be bitter. I spent my life doing just what he is doing, saving my own skin.

While he was walking home, the enormity of what he had done began to dawn on him. He had always had access to all the facts, of course. He had simply failed to combine them and realize their implications. Without the principal's endorsement, his report would cause serious repercussions. It might very well mean the loss of his job. There were rules for the protection of employees of long standing. But mofussil private schools had a way of getting around such rules.

He decided he would simply have to face the consequences. The loss of his job would not be such a great tragedy. He was only 3 years away from retirement anyway. His children were on their own, a daughter married and two sons in good jobs. For once in his life he was in a position to do something he felt was right, without fear of consequences. He was sick of doing the bidding of the petty politicians and maneuverers who ran the school, and of always being afraid of losing his job if he punished or failed their delinquent children. There had to come a time in every man's life when he had to square all these things with his conscience.

When he reached home he called out as usual, 'I am home'. While he removed his coat and had a wash, his wife would have a cup of tea ready for him. He debated telling her about what had happened, but discarded the idea. He had always been thankful for her unquestioning acceptances of his decisions, though her acceptance had meant only that she was not sufficiently interested. Since this time being he was content to leave it.

The reactions came sooner than he expected. Mr Thakar, the lawyer, brought up the subject during their before-dinner walk.

'Principal Deshpande asked me to have a talk with you', he said.

Mr Tagde said 'I have made my decision and nothing you say is going to change it'.

Mr Thakar looked at his friend in surprise.

'Wait till I have had my say', he said, holding up his hand. 'I hold no brief for Veerendra More. He is despicable and deserves to be kicked out of school. The point is this. You know and I know that your report is not going to serve that purpose, because of circumstances you know very well. Then why commit suicide needlessly?'

'I know you have only my interests at heart, and I am thankful for it. But it's no use your trying to talk me out of this. I have made up my mind'.

'But why?'

'I think this whole system is rotten, by which politicians control educational institutions. Somebody has to strike out against it'.

'Why you?'

'Why not me? Because I am just a poor insignificant teacher?'

Mr Thakar sighed.

'Think of the consequences. First, you may lose your job'.

'I wouldn't mind. I can continue to make a living by giving tuitions. That was what I had planned to do after my retirement anyway'.

'Do you think it would be easy for you to get tuitions if you declare yourself openly an enemy of the Mores?'

Mr Tagde was silent a long time. This was a logical possibility, but it had not occurred to him.

'Everybody in this town is not afraid of them', he said finally. 'And if they are, there are always other places to go to'.

'Oh, you mean you are prepared to disarrange your whole life over this worthless boy?'

'Yes'.

'Well, I admire you, Tagde but I still think you are making a foolish mistake'.

Vishnupant Joshi came to see him the next morning, large, aggressively hearty man, a Brahmin *bagaitdar*, careful of his skin but foxy enough to gain a foothold in Maratha politics, and therefore the ideal pacifier and go-between.

Over tea Mr Tagde said, 'Why should a father's money and political power protect his child from punishment which he richly deserves?'

Every time he argued his case, he seemed to receive an inner reinforcement from his own words.

'I agree with you, it shouldn't. But the fact is that it does. It does all the time, all over the world. We have to live with it. That's life. You have to keep your balance. Why jeopardise your position for a fine-sounding sentiment?'

'We are looking at the question from two opposing points of view, Mr Joshi, and I cannot hope to make you see mine'.

'Don't be in a hurry to take a stand. Think about it for a while. There is still time to withdraw your report?'

'You can take it as final that I will not withdraw it. If necessary, I am prepared to hand in my resignation'.

'You are aware that the school committee has powers to stop your pension?' 'I was not aware of it until you mentioned it'. Mr Tagde said in cold anger. 'If you came here to ensure my compliance through threats, you are wasting your time'.

On Wednesday night when Mr Tagde was returning home from a visit to the public lavatory which he used, he was attacked by a group of boys. They beat him with sticks and stones and fists. He thought he recognized Veerendra More among them, thought he heard his voice urging the others to 'teach the bastard a lesson'.

The next morning, covered with turmeric paste and bandages, unable to get up, Mr Tagde lay in bed groaning with pain.

The night before when he walked in after the meeting, his wife had been horrified and angry.

'Why won't you take back your silly report? Is it worth being beaten, losing your job? Oh yes, I know what's going on, even if you won't tell me anything'.

'I think it's worth it', he said calmly.

'They will kill you'.

'Let them. I am an old man, I am not afraid of dying'.

'You think only of yourself. What about me? What will happen to me if you die? I shall be a helpless widow for nothing'.

Mr Tagde felt like laughing.

He said gently, 'Not for nothing, my dear, for a principle'.

'What good will a principle be to me when I am a widow?'

Then he did laugh, and she withdrew into sullenness which she did not abandon with the dawning of the next day. Watching her going about her work silently, he thought I cannot be bothered with inessentials, now. I have jumped into this, and I will not back out. God will look after me, and look after her if something does happen to me.

Their neighbours had seen him coming home with a bloody face, so the news must be all over town, but nobody came to see him. This is what I shall have to stand alone. He thanked God for giving him this opportunity to become free of fear at last, to grow into a tall, proud man.

In the evening Mr Thakar came. 'Glad to see you'. Mr Tagde said, 'I thought you had also abandoned me, like the others'. 'Ha-ha, you do get funny ideas'.

Mr Tagde frowned at the lawyer's levity in the face of the seriousness of the situation.

'I bring you news', Mr Thakar said. 'Good or bad?' Mr Tagde asked cautiously. 'That depends on you'.

'If you are going to ask me to back out, you can save your breath'.

'At least let me tell you everything before you jump to conclusions. When I heard about the beating, I said to myself, this has gone too far. Something must be done about it. So I went to see Ramarao More, Veerendra's uncle. I put it to him that you were not going to withdraw your report no matter what, and many of the townspeople respected you for it; that the beating you had received was disgraceful and sufficient evidence, if any was needed, that your report is accurate; that the beating, if no action was taken about it, would create a lot of resentment in the town. Finally I said that if he looked at the thing rationally – I emphasized the point that I felt he was the only member of their family who was fully capable of thinking rationally – being kicked out of school might be the best thing that could happen to Veerendra. He agreed'.

'What! Mr Tagde shot up in bed'.

'Calm yourself. Of course he did not agree that Veerendra should be kicked out of school. He agreed that it would do Veerendra good to be taken out of school and put in a boarding school such as the Solapur boys' school which is run especially for problem boys. Naturally the family has not been happy about Veerendra's exploits, but they haven't known how to control him. I also brought it to Ramrao's attention that, in view of the forthcoming elections in which Veerendra's father is a candidate, any adverse publicity – such as you, I said, were capable of giving this matter – would be undesirable at this time. So he consulted with Veerendra's father, and they have agreed to take the boy out of school immediately, and in June, only three months from now, send him away. This is of course on condition that you withdraw the report about the boy immediately. You will have to agree that it is fair compromise because that gives you what you want'.

Mr Tagde, white and trembling, sank back on his pillow.

'What is the matter?' Mr Thakar asked in alarm. 'Are you feeling ill?'

'No, no, I am all right. This is such a surprise'.

'I understand. After the tension of the last few days, it must be a sudden relief. You do agree, don't you? I have to get in touch with Mr More and let him know tonight'.

Mr Tagde nodded mechanically and then closed his eyes; a tired, old teacher looking ahead to three more years of teaching and then retirement and a pension however measly.

GLOSSARY

Bagaitdar	:	A rich farmer
Conscience	:	Ethics
Delinquent	:	Disobedient
Despicable	:	Disgraceful
Extempore	:	Unplanned
Exultation	:	Happiness
Nondescript	:	Dull
Obscenity	:	Indecency
Pacifier	:	Peacemaker
Prank	:	Joke
Repercussion	:	Result
Unwavering	:	Consistent

COMPREHENSION QUESTIONS

I. Answer the following questions in about 200 words each.

1. Why does Mr Tagde decide to file a report against the More boy?
2. Why do you think the principal hesitated to approve Mr Tagde's report?
3. What is the outcome of Mr Tagde's action in the end? Write your comments.
4. Justify the title 'Death of a Hero'. Explain in detail.
5. What do you think about the boy More? Is he a prankster?
6. Write a character sketch of Mr Tagde.

II. Use the following idioms in your sentences. The first one is been done for you.

Idiom : Save one's breath
Meaning : To keep quiet, to refrain from talking
Example : I told her to *save her breath* as I didn't trust her anymore and did not believe in her stories either.

1. At the drop of a hat
2. Kick the bucket
3. Make a long story short
4. Spill the beans

III. Fill in the blanks with appropriate phrasal verbs from the following options.

1. I'm really tired because I ________ at 5 AM this morning.
   (a) got around
   (b) got up
   (c) got on
2. ________! Things will get better.
   (a) Cheer on
   (b) Cheer at
   (c) Cheer up
3. My car ________ on the freeway.
   (a) broke down
   (b) broke up
   (c) broke through
4. It's warm inside. _______your coat.
   (a) Take off
   (b) Take up
   (c) Take into
5. It's so loud here. Can you _______the radio a little?
   (a) turn down
   (b) turn up
   (c) turn out

IV. Think, Discuss and Respond.

1. If you were Mr Tagde, would you have responded in a similar manner initially?
2. How do you think Veerendra More responded to his family's decision in the end?
3. Is it difficult to be a Mr Tagde in today's world? Discuss.
4. According to you, what decision by the management would have settled the issue between the Mr Tagde and the More boy?

V. Writing Exercise

1. Try to recreate the story from Veerendra More's point of view.
2. Summarize the story in your own words.

Chapter Seven

The Doctor's Word

R.K. Narayan

R.K. *Narayan* (1906–2001), *an Indian author and journalist, is widely considered to be one of India's greatest English language novelists. He is known for his simple and unpretentious writing style. He is one of the three leading figures in English literature, along with Mulk Raj Anand and Raja Rao and is credited in bringing a new genre to the rest of the world. His popular works include* The English Teacher, The Financial Expert *and* Waiting for the Mahatma. *He was born in Madras in* 1906. *In* 1958, *Narayan's work* The Guide *won him the National prize of the Indian Literary Academy, the country's highest literary honour. He died at the age of* 95, *following a cardiorespiratory failure.*

The Doctor's Word *tells us how people blindly trust a doctor's word, and how it saves the life of a patient. Dr Raman was an experienced doctor and was known to always speak the truth. He did not believe in giving false hope to the patients. His word always was held in high esteem. Here in this story a situation comes up where his best friend Gopal is taken ill at his home and is hanging between life and death. But when he has to make a choice between his principles and relations, the relations dominate. Gopal survives because of Dr Raman's lie.*

People came to him when the patient was on his last legs. Dr Raman often burst out, 'Why couldn't you have come a day earlier?' The reason was obvious – visiting fee twenty-five rupees, and more than that, people liked to shirk the fact that the time had come to call in Dr Raman; for them there was something ominous in the very association. As a result, when the big man came on the scene it was always a quick decision one way or another. There was no scope or time for any kind of wavering or whitewashing. Long years of practice of this kind had bred in the doctor a certain curt truthfulness; for that very reason his opinion was valued; he was not a mere doctor expressing an opinion but a judge pronouncing a verdict. The patient's life hung on his words. This never unduly worried Dr Raman. He never believed that agreeable words ever saved lives. He did not think it was any of his business to provide comforting lies when, as a matter of course, nature would tell them truth in a few hours. However, when he glimpsed the faintest sign of hope, he rolled up his sleeve and stepped into the arena: it might be hours or days, but he never withdrew till he wrested the prize from Yama's hands.

Today, standing over a bed, the doctor felt that he himself needed someone to tell him soothing lies. He mopped his brow with his kerchief and sat down in the chair beside the bed. On the bed lay his dearest friend in the world, Gopal. They had known each other for 40 years now, starting with their kindergarten days. They could not, of course, meet as much as they wanted, each being wrapped in his own family and profession. Occasionally, on a Sunday, Gopal would walk into the consulting room and wait patiently in a corner till the doctor was free, and then they would dine together, see a picture and talk of each other's life and activities. It was a classic friendship, which endured untouched by changing times, circumstances and activities.

In his busy round of work, Dr Raman had not noticed that Gopal had not called in for over three months now. He only remembered it when he saw Gopal's son sitting on a bench in the consulting hall one crowded morning. Dr Raman could not talk to him for over an hour. When he got up and was about to pass on to the operating room, he called up the young man and asked, 'What brings you here, sir?' The youth was nervous and shy. 'Mother sent me here'.

'What can I do for you?'

'Father is ill ...'

It was an operation day and he was not free till three in the afternoon. He rushed off straight from the clinic to his friend's house, in Lawley Extension.

Gopal lay in bed as if in sleep. The doctor stood over him and asked Gopal's wife, 'How long has he been in bed?'

'A month and a half, Doctor'.

'Who is attending him?'

'A doctor in the next street. He comes down once in three days and gives him medicine'.

'What is his name?' He had never heard of him. 'Someone I don't know, but I wish he had the goodness to tell me about it. Why, why couldn't you have sent me word earlier?'

'We thought you would be busy and did not wish to trouble you unnecessarily'. They were apologetic and miserable. There was hardly any time to be lost. He took off his coat and opened his bag. He took out an injection tube; the needle sizzled over the stove. The sick man's wife whimpered in a corner and essayed to ask questions.

'Please don't ask questions', snapped the doctor. He looked at the children, who were watching the sterilizer, and said, 'Send them all away somewhere, except the eldest'.

He shot in the drug, sat back in his chair and gazed at the patient's face for over an hour. The patient still remained motionless. The doctor's face gleamed with perspiration, and his eyelids dropped with fatigue. The sick man's wife stood in a corner and watched silently. She asked timidly, 'Doctor, shall I make some coffee for you?' 'No', he replied, although he felt famished, having missed his mid-day meal. He got up and said, 'I will be back in a few minutes. Don't disturb him on any account'. He picked up his bag and went to his car. In a quarter of an hour he was back, followed by an assistant and a nurse. The doctor told the lady of the house, 'I have to perform an operation'.

'Why, why? Why?' she asked faintly.

'I will tell you all that soon. Will you leave your son here to help us, and go over to the next house and stay there till I call you?'

The lady felt giddy and sank down on the floor, unable to bear the strain. The nurse attended to her and led her out.

At about eight in the evening, the patient opened his eyes and stirred slightly in bed. The assistant was overjoyed. He exclaimed enthusiastically, 'Sir, he will pull through'. The doctor looked at him coldly and whispered, 'I would give anything to see him pull through but, but the heart …'

'The pulse has improved, Sir'.

'Well, well', replied the doctor. 'Don't trust it. It is only a false flash-up, very common in these cases'. He ruminated for a while and added, 'If the pulse keeps up till eight in the morning, it will go on for the next 40 years, but I doubt very much if we shall see anything of it at all after two tonight'.

He sent away the assistant and sat beside the patient. At about eleven, the patient opened his eyes and smiled at his friend. He showed a slight improvement. He was able to take in a little food. A great feeling of relief and joy went through the household. They swarmed around the doctor and poured out their gratitude. He sat in his seat beside the bed, gazing sternly at the patient's face, hardly showing any signs of hearing what they were saying to him. The sick man's wife asked, 'Is he now out of danger?' Without turning his head the doctor said, 'give glucose and brandy every forty minutes; just a couple of spoons will do'. The lady went away to the kitchen. She felt she must know the truth whatever it was. Why was the great man so evasive? The suspense was unbearable. Perhaps he could not speak so near the patient's bed. She beckoned to him from the kitchen doorway. The doctor bit his lips and replied, looking at the floor, 'Don't get excited. Unless you must know about it, don't ask now'. Her eyes opened wide in terror. She clasped her hands together and implored, 'tell me the truth'. The doctor replied, 'I would rather not talk to you now'. He turned round and went back to his chair. A terrible wailing shot through the still house; the patient stirred and looked about in bewilderment. The doctor got up again, went over to the kitchen door, drew it in securely and shut off the wall.

When the doctor resumed his seat, the patient in the faintest whisper possible, 'Is that someone crying?' The doctor advised, 'Don't exert yourself. You mustn't talk'. He felt the pulse. It was already agitated by the exertion. The patient asked, 'Am I going? Don't hide it from me'.

The doctor made a deprecating noise and sat back in his chair. He had never faced a situation like this. It was not in his nature to whitewash. People attached great value to his word because of that. He stole a look at the other. The patient motioned a finger to draw him nearer and whispered, 'I must know how long I am going to last. I must sign the will. It is all ready. Ask my wife for the dispatch box. You must sign as a witness'.

'Oh!' the doctor exclaimed. 'You are exerting yourself too much. You must be quieter'. He felt idiotic to be repeating it. 'How fine it would be', he reflected, 'to drop the whole business and run away somewhere without answering anybody any question!' The patient clutched the doctor's wrist with his weak fingers and said, 'Ramu, it is my good fortune that you are here at this moment. I can trust your word. I can't leave my property unsettled. That will mean endless misery for my wife and children. You know all about Subbaiah and his gang. Let me sign before it is too late. Tell me …'

'Yes, presently', replied the doctor. He walked off to his car, sat in the back seat and reflected. He looked at his watch. Midnight, if the will was to be signed, it must be done within the next two hours, or never. He could not be responsible for a mess there; he knew the family affairs too well and about those wolves, Subbaiah and his gang. But what could he do? If he asked him to sign the will, it would virtually mean a death sentence and destroy the thousandth part of a chance that the patient had of survival. He got down from the car and went in. He resumed his seat in the chair. The patient was staring at him appealingly. The doctor said to himself, 'If my word can save his life, he shall not die. The will be damned'. He called, 'Gopal, listen'. This was the first time he was going to do a piece of acting before a patient, simulate a feeding and conceal his judgement. He stopped over the patient and said, with deliberate emphasis, 'Don't worry about the will now. You are going to live. Your heart is absolutely sound'. A new glow suffused the patient's face as he heard it. He asked in a tone of relief, 'Do you say so? If it comes from your lips it must be true …'

The doctor said, 'Quite right. You are improving every second. Sleep in peace. You must not exert yourself on any account. You must sleep very soundly. I will see you in the morning'. The patient looked at him gratefully for a moment and then closed his eyes. The doctor picked up his bag and went out, shutting the door softly behind him.

On his way home he stopped for a moment at his hospital, called out his assistant and said, 'That Lawley Extension case. You might expect the collapse any second now. Go there with a tube of … in hand, and give it in case the struggle is too hard at the end. Hurry up'.

Next morning he was back at Lawley Extension at 10. From his car he made a dash for the sick bed. The patient was awake and looked very well. The assistant reported satisfactory pulse. The doctor put his tube to his heart, listened for a while and told the sick man's wife, 'Don't look so unhappy, lady. Your husband will live to be ninety'. When they were going back to the hospital, the assistant sitting beside him in the car asked, 'Is he going to live, sir?'

'I will bet on it. He will live to be ninety. He has turned the corner. How he has survived this attack will be a puzzle to me all my life', replied the doctor.

GLOSSARY

Appealingly	:	In a pleasing manner
Bewilderment	:	Confusion resulting from failure to understand
Curt	:	Brief and to the point
Deprecating	:	Tendency to diminish
Emphasis	:	Special importance or significance
Endured	:	Put up with something
Evasive	:	Deliberately vague or ambiguous
Exerting	:	Too much of work
Fatigue	:	Temporary loss of strength and energy
Gazing	:	A long fixed look
Glimpsed	:	A quick look
Implored	:	Call politely
Mopped	:	Clean or soak up liquid from (something) by wiping
Ominous	:	Threatening
Shirk	:	Avoid

Suffused	:	Get a ray of hope
Sternly	:	Strictly
Timidly	:	In a shy manner
Whimpered	:	Cry weakly or softly
Wrested	:	Obtain by seizing forcibly

COMPREHENSION QUESTIONS

I. Answer the following questions in about one or two words each.

1. When does Dr Raman realize that he hasn't seen Gopal for a long time?
2. What does Dr Raman realize after seeing Gopal?
3. How long has Gopal been ill?
4. Does Dr Raman's word come true in Gopal's case?

II. Answer the following questions in about 100 words each.

1. Describe briefly the relation between the doctor and the patient.
2. What is Dr Raman's image in the village?
3. Gopal's wish regarding the will was not accepted by Dr Raman. Why?
4. Describe the character of the doctor.

III. Answer the following questions in 200–250 words each.

1. 'The Doctor's Word' is the story of the relationship between a doctor and a patient. Do you agree?
2. Sketch the character of Dr Raman.

IV. Use the following idioms in your own sentences. The first one is done for you.

Idiom : Raining cats and dogs
Meaning : Very heavy rainfall
Example : It is *raining cats and dogs.*

1. Add insult to injury
2. At the drop of a hat
3. Back to the drawing board
4. Bite off more than you can chew
5. Blessing in disguise

6. Cost an arm and a leg
7. Every cloud has a silver lining

V. Use the following phrasal verbs in your own sentences. The first one is done for you.

Phrasal verb : Back out
Meaning : To withdraw
Example : She *backed out* from the committee.

1. Back up
2. Blow up
3. Call on someone
4. Drop out
5. Get away
6. Go through
7. Kick off

Chapter Eight

The Ultimate Weapon

(Brahmastram)

Abburi Chaya Devi

Abburi Chaya Devi is a noted Telugu fiction writer who hails from an affluent family of writers. Her husband Abburi Varadarajeshwara Rao was also a writer and critic. He also served as the Chairman of Official Languages Commission. Abburi Chaya Devi also served as a librarian at the Jawaharlal Nehru University, New Delhi, in the 1960s. Her major works include Anaga Anaga, Abburi Chaya Devikathalu, Mirthunjaya, Tana Margam, Mana Jeevithalu, Jiddu Krishnamurthy Vyakhyanalu, Parichita Lekha *and* Bonsai Batukulu. *She was awarded the Central Sahitya Akademi Award for her work* Tana Margam *in 2005. She has also received other honours such as Ranganayakamma Puraskaram in 2003 and Telugu University Award in 1996. She has also served as a member of the General Council of Sahitya Akademi from 1998 to 2002.*

The story is about an ordinary Indian woman who in spite of all her accomplishments still is faced with so many constraints laid out by the patriarchal set up of our society. The story appeared in her anthology of short stories entitled Tana Margam *in Telugu. It is translated into English by Dr C. Vijayashree and Dr G.K. Subbarayudu.*

Eating Cream and Butter as a Child

(sometimes … evading mother's observant eyes)

Hiding behind the door like a kitten when scolded by father occasionally – except these, I have had no relationship or connection with a cat since childhood.

A cat used to sleep in the hearth in the afternoon in my house. My mother used to boil milk in the morning and take out the milk pot from the hearth and keep it in the kitchen around 10 O'clock. After the fires dowsed completely the cat would go and sleep in the hearth till the night. I don't remember the colour of the skin of that cat. I never observed it properly. No one ever called and offered milk to that cat. There were some bandicoots in our compound, but no rats in our house. I don't know what that cat fed on.

My mother was orthodox and observed lots of restrictions. So no cats or dogs were ever allowed into our house. That does not mean my mother did not have compassion for animals. Early in the morning, one day, my mother was churning butter milk, singing wake-up songs. She heard some loud splashing sound from the well so early, she went into the backyard. She heard the mewing of the cat from the well. The cat had fallen into the well and was clinging to the side walls of the well. My mother took pity on the cat, put the bucket into the well and after the cat clutched at the rope, gently pulled it out. As mother was about to reach out to the bucket, the scared cat bit her hand and fled. When we woke up, we found mother sitting with her hand in a bandage. Some home remedy was applied. After a couple of days the wound got infected and pus collected there. She had a fever too. Father fetched a doctor. Mother suffered from pain and fever for quite some time. For a month, she was bedridden.

From that time, I developed a phobia for cats. Not only was I afraid that it might sneak into the kitchen and polish off milk or curd but also scared that it might bite me, if I ever went near it. Except scaring a cat with a stick from a distance, I never went anywhere near one.

Recently, after my retirement, we moved into our own house. The house was neat and spacious. We got a mesh fixed to the doors and windows as a protection against flies and mosquitoes. I do not know how they managed, but small rats used to come in. Though we kept all the drains firmly closed, they found some gap somewhere and sneaked in. From the banana offerings of my mother-in-law's deities to plastic containers in my kitchen, they bit holes into everything. The newspapers on the table, books in the almirah too had come in for a torture. We kept a rat trap with a bait of bread crumbs and vegetable pieces. But the rats came nowhere near the trap. We made tasty snacks and tried to attract rats into the trap. One or two greedy ones got trapped but the rest gave us a 'we know your tricks' look and ran away swiftly. While we entertained guests in the drawing room, rats freely ran to and fro causing us embarrassment. Someone advised me to mix poison in food and keep it in places frequented by rats. I was not ready to follow this advice. If a dead rat lies in some corner unnoticed the house will stink. 'Why all this hassle? The little ones are moving about the house adding to its glitter, let them be', I was prepared to persuade myself.

But my mother-in-law was not ready for such reconciliation. 'How useless are you! Can't you control those stupid rats? If you get a cat in for a couple of days, all the rats will simply vanish', she said.

'Come and stay with us for a couple of days' – if you invite thus which cat will oblige? It might come on its own terms. But our house is secured with mesh doors and windows. No scope for any intrusion. How will any cat dare to enter a prison-like house? Even if I want to bring a cat from neighbourhood, I do not have the guts to approach a cat.

'How strange, amma! If you just catch hold of a cat and show him the rat, won't it simply grab the rat in its mouth and run away?' my mother-in-law would say as if it were as easy as unwrapping a chocolate and eating it.

Sensing my discomfiture, my husband said, 'There's a kitten in Suryarao's house. I'll ask him to leave it in our house for a couple of days'. They agreed, I believe, but they never brought their kitten to our house.

One afternoon, while I was standing in the balcony, I saw a kitten shimmering amidst the plants at some distance. I immediately said, 'Mew! Mew! Come!' extending a friendly hand. It quickly withdrew, hid behind the plants and began to throw nervous glances at me. I went into the kitchen at once, brought a saucer of milk, kept in the balcony for the kitten to see, and called it again, 'Come!' It did not move even one step forward but kept staring at me. I spilt a few drops of milk on the floor to attract its attention and said, 'See! Milk for you! Come!' Now it looked curious, but did not budge from its place. Then I tried another strategy.

I left the saucer in the balcony, went inside, closed the door rather ajar and started observing through the gap. The kitten, having decided that there was no one around, came out of its hiding slowly, walking in slow measured steps, looking around carefully, approached the balcony. Standing at some distance, it stared at the saucer. I made no noise. Then it came forward, and smelled the milk bringing its mouth close to the saucer. Then it started drinking milk.

From that day onwards, it used to come into the garden every day and look at the balcony. If I happened to notice it, I used to keep a saucer of milk for it in the balcony. After my withdrawal from there, it would come, drink the milk and leave licking its lips. On one occasion while it was drinking milk, I slowly opened the door and took a couple of steps into the balcony. It stopped drinking the milk, turned back and looked at me. I stood motionless. Maybe it felt assured that I would do no harm, it continued drinking the milk.

One day, children playing in the neighbourhood tried to catch that kitten. It sprang into our balcony and hid behind a flower pot. Noticing this I went close to it. I was not scared by that little kitten sitting buddle in fear behind the pot. I felt sympathetic. I sat down and touched it softly on its back. It folded up further and moved back a little. I became bolder, and began stroking it on its back. The children in the street, who were chasing it, gathered at the gate and asked me, 'Is that kitten yours, aunty?'

'How I wish it were ours!' I thought to myself but said outwardly, 'Yes'.

'What's its name?' they asked.

'Its name … Browny', I said promptly. That kitten was in light brown colour; that's why I thought of that name at once.

The time of christening must have been auspicious; Browny consented to come into my house. Every time it came into the balcony and mewed, I would open the door. Initially a little apprehensive, then quite boldly, it would come in. I would keep the saucer of milk outside the kitchen, and it would drink the milk. By and by, I began to offer it milk and rice or curd rice. Later I would keep it in my lap and chat with it stroking its head, neck and back. It would allow me do that for any length of time. When I stroked its neck, it would lift its neck like a kid, like a calf, as if it was asking me to caress it properly. If I stopped chattering and kept stroking silently, it would lift its head and look at me as if it was asking me why I stopped talking to it.

Its mouth looked like a curved line drawn with a red pencil. Its neck and belly were soft like white silk. If I touched its belly, maybe it felt tickled; it would sit up straight and lick its body. As if it was absorbed in some urgent work, it would lick its own body, sitting in my lap, yet ignoring my presence. Wetting its hand (front paw) with its own saliva, it would clean itself – face, ears and cheeks.

One day, while it was sitting in my lap, I saw a rat scurrying under the almirah. I jumped to my feet and left the kitten near the almirah. It ran from here to there in utter confusion. I picked up an umbrella from a corner and rattled it under the almirah. The rat scrambled out and flitted along the wall to another corner.

'There … a rat! Catch … catch it', I yelled at Browny. My yelling, the rattling noise of the umbrella, the scurrying rat made Browny even more panicky, and it tried to escape the scene. But the windows and the doors were all shut; and Browny ran from one room to another for shelter from some catastrophe.

Watching this entire spectacle, my mother-in-law asked me with amusement, 'From where did you obtain a cat that's scared of a rat, girlie?' For the past week she'd been observing me feed milk and rice to the kitten, and dandling it in my lap, telling it stories. 'A cat must be left where there are rats … not fed well and fondled', she'd said, squeezing her cheeks in amazement. Now, when the kitten made no attempt to get the rat, she seemed to be mocking at me.

A while later, I began searching the rooms for Browny. No trace of it. Wondering if it had tucked itself away under the divan in the drawing room I bent low and called 'Where are you, Browny?'

'Uumh', it mewed as if saying 'here I am'. Whether it understood that 'Browny' meant her, or recognized my voice, I don't know … but I felt quite elated. I opened the door saying, 'Enough achieved for today now, out!' Browny scampered out with a 'meeoww' for a thank you.

Though it did not catch any mice, it felt as if there was a little less of the pest because Browny went about home with a meeoww on its lips. If there was a slight delay in giving it milk, it would get into a tangle with your steps crying meeoww. I'd get mighty pleased, as if it had said 'Mama'.

However, mother-in-law did not like Browny roaming about the house like it owned the place. Mother-in-law's previous complaint was that rats nibbled through the plantains kept as offering at worship in the pooja room. Now it was the kitten that toppled the figurines of gods in her *mandiram*. A regular racket ensued. If the kitten so much as peeped into her room, mother-in-law chased it out with a cane and some grunts.

Browny never stayed at home at night. Throughout the day, however, it slept under my cot or under the divan in the drawing room. If someone rang the doorbell it would prance around me, getting in my way. As I moved apace to answer the door, it'd leap and run off to some corner the moment it caught sight of the person at the entrance.

One day, as I lay in bed reading, there was huge commotion. When I peered, I saw Browny, a rat in her mouth, running around in panic. I cried out loudly in jubilation, 'Hey! Watch … watch … Browny has caught a rat'. My mother-in-law and my husband rushed out to see what was happening. My screaming and their rushing in scared Browny even more and it withdrew deeper under the almirah. Worried that it might kill and eat the rat there itself, I opened the door to send it out. But Browny did not heed my calls. Mother-in-law rattled her walking stick under the metallic monster. Browny was terrified and quickly emerged with the rat grit in its teeth. And, instead of escaping from the front door, it rushed into my mother-in-law's room and went under her almirah! Mother-in-law was now furious, and rattled her walking stick. Browny was hurt and scampered out leaving the limp rat behind. I picked up the half-dead rat with a broom and threw it away outside.

On another day Browny seemed suffering a bout of vomiting … don't know what it had eaten outside. I took her out into the backyard and watched over anxiously. She sniffed around a bit and then went about chewing some grass. I didn't know before that the cats also ate grass. Soon after, Browny threw up. In a while it recovered. Did not lap up the milk I gave. It slurped some water stagnant near the bathroom drain and slipped into slumber, entirely drained.

After that incident, Browny did not drink enough milk. It began to lose weight and becoming skinny. Not knowing what to feed her, how to fatten her, I bought and read an English book on cats. It had a wealth of information on all basic issues, and the nature and behaviour of cats as well.

On any occasion, if a thin stream of water flowed twisting and turning on the floor, Browny would sit at a distance, still and straight, and watch as if it was some strange, fascinating event. Then it would run in the direction of the flow and stare with utter focus, 'See how, it watches; it's so adorable when doing this', I'd say, calling my husband's attention. I thought it was my Browny's special trait. The book described this as a common pattern among cats. Hanging by the flounces of door curtains, leaping at any rope or thread that hung free; playing with something like football with small objects such as a bottle cap, pencil or a ball were some adorable tricks of Browny.

If they couldn't digest what had been eaten they'd chew grass and cure themselves of indigestion; usually they took care of their health issues themselves; cats are naturally inclined to cleanliness; they licked their bodies clean and resisted any ones attempts to bathe them; they dug out soil with their paws, defecated in those little trenches and covered them up with the dugout soil. I learnt many such things, which I had not observed, from the book. I also learnt how to detect the gender of the cat, boy or girl... from the book. Our Browny is a pussy cat, a girl.

If I showed any affection for the cat occasionally, mother-in-law fumed like smoke from burnt seasoning in the kitchen.

'Should not take cat for a pet. Will go blind', she said one day.

'Heard that cat shuts eyes when drinking milk. Never that taking it for a pet would lead to blindness', I shot back.

'Ayyoo! You don't know. Cat always prays that the owner go blind', she insisted.

'Crazy little bastard! Where would it have so many thoughts from!' I laughed. With that she began grumbling 'I'm not half worth that wretched cat', turning towards her room.

She started believing that her gradual loss of vision was thanks to the cat. Browny never let go of us, though I tried to get rid of her for the sake of my mother-in-law's sentiments. When I answered the door, Browny wriggled in through the smallest opening and got entailed with my steps. If I sat in a chair, it'd jump into my lap. If I lay in bed, it'd snuggle close to the pillow.

One day my husband kept a clean white dhoti on the bed preparing for his bath. Browny went and curled up on the white dhoti. As he came out of his bath, he began yelling loudly. I ran up to the scene from the kitchen in alarm. 'Throw out this stupid cat, bloody nuisance. The more I keep discreet silence, the more you raise him head-high', he bawled. Mother-in-law sang chorus to his voice. Browny meanwhile, slept without stir, peacefully as on a feather bed. 'Up! Browny', I said, tapping the cat. It curled up more giving me one look as if saying 'I like it here, I won't move', and slept. I picked up Browny by the scruff of its neck, and in helpless anger threw it out of the balcony into the lawn. As I went in and latched the door, Browny came in like lightning and cringed at my feet.

Mother-in-law made to her room, scowling and gesturing, murmuring, 'Now it's done … the great farce'.

Another evening I went across in the neighbourhood to attend a *seemantham* function – a customary seventh month celebratory ritual for an expecting young woman. It was more than an hour before the function was completed. It got pretty dark as I returned home. When I pressed the calling bell, my husband opened the door bellowing and booming. Didn't understand a word of what he said. I stepped in rather apprehensively asking, 'What happened?'

I was afraid my mother-in-law suffered high BP due to the delay in serving dinner. But she was watching from behind a slightly drawn curtain of the drawing room!

'Did Browny spoil something?' I asked shrivelling a little with guilt.

He thundered now, 'Do you know where you left the cat?'

I did not get it at all; 'keep it … where? After cooking dinner, I didn't even check for Browny in that hurry to go for the function', I snivelled.

'Precisely that … no need to check? Enough to dress up and leave?' withering sarcasm in tone. Mother-in-law's chorus was more pronounced. 'Unnecessarily *Brahma Hatya Paatakam* would have been our dreadful lot', she drawled. I was fuming now. 'But what the hell happened?' I barked.

'You locked the damned cat in the almirah and went away. I heard its cries and the racket and opened the door … so it is okay. Otherwise bloody thing would be dead by now. Would we dream that it was in the almirah? Searched all over the house. Then I almost died of exhaustion searching for the almirah keys', he gasped.

'Ayyayyo! Must have climbed into the almirah when I opened it for the *pattu* sari. I didn't observe … where's Browny?' I asked anxiously.

'Leave Browny for the moment … first do something about that almirah; it has soiled all the clothes inside. Next time such a thing happens, I'll throw it out onto the street, and you too', he warned and stormed out into the street.

I went in and opened the almirah door. All clothes in the lowest shelf were as if ransacked. As I drew them out to stack up again a stench followed. Looked like it had defecated on those clothes, out of fear … the clothes were also wet. I took them out into the balcony and dumped them in the bucket for washing. Then cleaned the entire almirah with phenyl, dried it, and washed all the clothes, by which time my back was broken.

Before this incident I had never seen Browny go with affection to anyone except me. Mother-in-law simply frightened her off by raising her walking stick. Husband always shooed it off saying 'Go away'. Now, after this fracas, Browny began traipsing about my husband's footsteps. I saw him even feed milk once to Browny … something I'd never seen before.

When a cat rubs its skin against ours and gambols around us it gives us a feel of its expression of love. Our hearts melt like butter in that warmth. As we try to return that love, holding it like a baby, it struggles and leaps off. If it nudges close to skin, we have to give milk or something to nibble. Or sit close to it and caress its neck and back. It does not accept any expression more demonstrative than this.

Since husband stopped shooing it away, Browny got enough courage to sit in the drawing room. Even when guests came it wouldn't budge. Little children, however, frightened her, and it would scamper away. The harder they tried to get hold of her, the more frightened she got and hid in some corner.

Browny liked salt biscuits, fried noodle, fried dal vadas, and other crunchy snacks. Before offering snacks, to anyone, one must put some of the snacks on the floor for her to enjoy. Otherwise it would leap up to the plates for its share.

Petting Browny like this vexed mother-in-law … she felt as if her skin stung due to an application of chilly and pepper. In this instance she is even more irritated that my husband is in it with me.

One afternoon, when I entered her room with some Horlicks, I found mother-in-law in bed looking blankly at the ceiling, as though recalling the past. Right hand was on her chest, left stretched out …

'Here. Take some Horlicks', I said.

'Leave it there', she said, continuing to stare into the blankness.

'Have it quickly. It will get cold', I said and came out of her room. Even as I went into the kitchen and stepped out again, she let out a shrill shriek. I ran into her room, terrified that she may have tipped the glass of hot Horlicks over herself. Her left hand middle finger was bleeding profusely. I was stunned by the sight. She was wailing.

'What happened in this little time?' I asked, looking left and right. At that very moment Browny emerged from under the bed and ran away in a flash.

'That cat-bitch hates me! See how it has bitten me.'

I examined her finger. Looked as if Browny's nails had scratched deep. Not a bite, I thought. Immediately I rinsed the wound with cotton dipped in Dettol, applied some Terramycin ointment, and put a bandage on the finger. Then I called husband and informed him. When he returned, he brought a doctor along. The doctor gave an anti-tetanus injection and left with the reassuring words 'Nothing to worry about *bammagaru.* In a little while the pain will subside … no fears'.

Anger with Browny resurfaced in him. 'Will you send the damned thing out of our house or not?' he demanded insistently.

'Even if I sent it away, it comes back, doesn't it … what should I do?'

'If you don't give it milk, it will go away on its own. If you make and feed it fried noodles, boondhi and pakori, why will it go? Decide once and for all whether it stays or I stay in this house', he grunted and stormed out.

I took Browny by its collar, sent it out and shut the door. Then slumped in a chair holding my head in both hands.

In less than ten minutes I heard the meeooww. I turned my head to a side and looked at the door. On the other side of the mesh door stood Browny with a baleful expression.

'*Mai… aavoon*?' she said.

As a reflex I almost jumped up from the chair to open the door. Promptly husband's threat to leave home held me back like a *Brahmastra*, the ultimate weapon. I slumped back in the chair weakly … and said '*nahii*' helplessly.

GLOSSARY

Gambols	:	Gay or light-hearted recreational activity for amusement
Hassle	:	Angry disturbance or disorderly fighting
Hearth	:	An open recess on the wall at the base of the chimney where fire can be built
Orthodox	:	Adhering to what is commonly accepted
Scrambled	:	Throw together in a disorderly fashion

COMPREHENSION QUESTIONS

I. Answer the following questions in about 500 words each.

1. Comment on the significance of the title of the short story 'The Ultimate Weapon' or 'Brahmastram'.
2. Explain the relationship between the protagonist and the kitten as portrayed in the short story 'The Ultimate Weapon'.
3. Do you think the short story reflects the plight of an average ordinary Indian woman? Explain.
4. Summarize the story in your own words.

II. Use the following idioms in your own sentences.

1. A couch potato
2. Like a bolt from the blue
3. Once in a blue moon
4. Out of the blue
5. To let the cat out of the bag
6. To pour/throw cold water on something

Chapter Nine

The Open Window

Saki

Hector *Hugh Munro or Saki* (18 Dec. 1870–14 Nov. 1916) *was a satirist and author with a taste for the witty and outrageous. Saki was a student of European history and gifted with a prodigious memory. If he had continued to write historical tracts, it is not improbable that the study of history would be looked upon today as a rather light endeavour. He wrote most of his best work for newspapers such as the* Westminster Gazette, Daily Express, Bystander, Morning Post *and* Outlook. *He was eminently capable of saving an entire discipline from a doddering reputation. His varied interests are apparent in his political satires, short stories and plays. He wrote political satires for the* Westminster Gazette, *and in* 1900 *he published* The Rise of the Russian Empire, *a serious historical work.*

After acting as foreign correspondent for the Morning Post *in the Balkans, Russia and Paris, in* 1908 *he settled in London, writing short stories and sketches:* Reginald (1904), Reginald in Russia (1910), The Chronicles of Clovis (1912) *and* Beasts and Super-Beasts (1914). *His most frequently anthologized works are* 'Tobermory', 'The Open Window', 'Sredni Vashtar', 'Laura' *and* 'The Schartz-Metterklume Method'. *His novel* The Unbearable Bassington (1912) *describes the adventures of a fastidious and likable but maladjusted hero, in a manner anticipating that of the early work of the English satirist Evelyn Waugh Munro was killed in action in World War* I.

'The Open Window' *is Saki's most popular short story. It was first collected in* Beasts and Super-Beasts *in* 1914. *Saki's wit is at the height of its power in this story of a spontaneous practical joke played upon a visiting stranger. The practical joke recurs in many of Saki's stories, but* 'The Open Window' *is perhaps his most successful and best known example of the type. Saki dramatizes here the conflict between reality and imagination, demonstrating how difficult it can be to distinguish between the two. Both the unfortunate Mr Nuttel and the reader fall victim to the story's joke, The reader is at first inclined to laugh at Nuttel for being so gullible. However, the reader, too, has been taken in by Saki's story and must come to the realization that he or she is also inclined to believe a well-told and interesting tale.*

'My aunt will come down very soon, Mr Nuttel', said a very calm young lady of 5 years of age, 'meanwhile you must try to bear my company'. Framton Nuttel tried to say something which would please the niece now present, without annoying the aunt who was about to come. He was supposed to be going through a cure for his nerves, but he doubted whether these polite visits to a number of total strangers would help much.

'I know how it will be', his sister had said when he was preparing to go away into the country. 'You will lose yourself down there and not speak to a living soul, and your nerves will be worse than ever through loneliness. I shall just give you letters of introduction to all the people I know there. Some of them, as far as I can remember, were quite nice'.

Framton wondered whether Mrs Sappleton, the lady to whom he was bringing one of the letters of introduction, was one of the nice ones.

'Do you know many of the people round here?' asked the niece, when she thought that they had sat long enough in silence.

'Hardly one', said Framton. 'My sister was staying here, you know, about four years ago, and she gave me letters of introduction to some of the people here'.

He made the last statement in a sad voice.

'Then you know almost nothing about my aunt?' continued the calm young lady. 'Only her name and address', Framton admitted. He was wondering whether Mrs Sappleton was married; perhaps she had been married and her husband was dead. But there was something of a man in the room.

'Her great sorrow came just three years ago', said the child. 'That would be after your sister's time'.

'Her sorrow?' asked Framton. Somehow, in this restful country place, sorrows seemed far away.

'You may wonder why we keep that window wide open on an October afternoon', said the niece, pointing to a long window that opened like a door on to the grass outside.'It is quite warm for the time of the year', said Framton, 'but has that window got anything to do with your aunt's sorrow?'

'Out through that window, exactly three years ago, her husband and her two young brothers went off for their day's shooting. They never came back. In crossing the country to the shooting ground, they were all three swallowed in a bog. It had been that terrible wet summer, you know, and places that were safe in other years became suddenly dangerous. Their bodies were never found. That was the worst part of it'. Here the child's voice lost its calm sound and became almost human. 'Poor aunt always thinks that they will come back some day, they and the little brown dog that was lost with them, and walk in at that window just as they used to do. That is why the window is kept open every evening till it is quite dark. Poor dear aunt, she has often told me how they went out, her husband with his white coat over his arm, and Ronnie, her youngest brother, singing a song, as he always did to annoy her, because she said it affected her nerves. Do you know, sometimes on quiet evenings like this, I almost get a strange feeling that they will all walk in through the window…'

She stopped and trembled. It was a relief to Framton when the aunt came busily into the room and apologized for being late.

'I hope Vera has been amusing you?' she said.

'She has been very interesting', said Framton.

'I hope you don't mind the open window', said Mrs Sappleton brightly. 'My husband and brothers will be home soon from shooting, and they always come in this way. They've been shooting birds today near the bog, so they'll make my poor carpets dirty. All you men do that sort of thing, don't you?'

She talked on cheerfully about the shooting and the scarcity of birds, and the hopes of shooting in the winter. To Framton, it was all quite terrible. He made a great effort, which was only partly successful, to turn the talk on to a more cheerful subject. He was conscious that his hostess was giving him only a part of her attention, and her eyes were frequently looking past him to the open window and the grass beyond. It was certainly unfortunate that he should have paid his visit on this sorrowful day.

'The doctors agree in ordering me complete rest, no excitement and no bodily exercise', said Framton, who had the common idea that total strangers want to know the least detail of one's illnesses, their cause and cure. 'On the matter of food, they are not so much in agreement', he continued.

'No?' said Mrs Sappleton in a tired voice. Then she suddenly brightened into attention – but not to what Framton was saying.

'Here they are at last!' she cried, 'just in time for tea, and don't they look as if they were muddy up to the eyes!'

Framton trembled slightly and turned towards the niece with a look intended to show sympathetic understanding.

The child was looking out through the open window with fear in her eyes. With a shock Framton turned round in his seat and looked in the same direction. In the increasing darkness, three figures were walking across the grass towards the window; they all carried guns under their arms, and one of them had also a white coat hung over his shoulders. A tired brown dog kept close at their heels. Noiselessly they drew near to the house, and then a young voice started to sing in the darkness.

Framton wildly seized his hat and stick; he ran out through the front door and through the gate. He nearly ran into a man on a bicycle.

'Here we are, my dear', said the bearer of the white coat, coming in through the window, 'fairly muddy, but most of it's dry. Who was that who ran out as we came up?'

'A most extraordinary man, a Mr Nuttel', said Mrs Sappleton. 'He could only talk about his illnesses, and ran off without a word of goodbye or apology when you arrived. One would think he had seen a ghost'.

'I expect it was the dog', said the niece calmly. 'He told me he had a terrible fear of dogs. He was once hunted into a graveyard somewhere in India by a lot of wild dogs, and had to spend the night in a newly dug grave with the creatures just above him. Enough to make anyone lose their nerve'.

She was very clever at making up stories quickly.

GLOSSARY

Bury oneself : Keep away from people
Cemetery : Piece of land where dead bodies are buried
Creepy feeling : Feeling of fear or uneasiness
Dazed : Unable to think
Engulf : Swallow up
Formal : According to accepted rules or customs
French window : Glass door opening
Marsh : Low-lying, wet land
Moor : Wild, hilly land
Nerve cure : Treatment for nervous disorder
Prospect : Hope of something happening
Rectory : House of the rector
Romance : Fanciful story
Self-possessed : Calm, confident
Spaniel : A kind of dog with long hair and long ears
Speciality : Something that a person does very well

COMPREHENSION QUESTIONS

I. Answer the following questions in about one or two words each.

1. Who is the main character?
2. What is the prevailing mood in this story?
3. What is the essential effect?

4. Did you find out whether Mrs Sappleton's husband and brother were present?
5. At what point do we exactly know whether the story is true or false?
6. What is the common point between Mr Framton Nuttel and the reader?

II. Answer the following questions in about 50 words each.

1. Why had Framton Nuttel come to the 'rural retreat'?
2. Why had his sister given him letters of introduction to people living there?
3. What had happened in the Sappleton family as narrated by the niece?
4. Why did Frampton rush out wildly?
5. The horror on the girl's face made Framton swing around in his seat. What did he see?

III. Answer the following questions in about 200–250 words each.

1. Sum up the short story bringing into relief the characters, the facts and the end of the story.
2. Justify the title. Explain with special emphasis on the part played by the open window.
3. With examples, explain the irony in the short story.
4. Rephrase the main ideas of the story in your own words.
5. Explain why you liked or disliked this short story by Saki.

IV. Use the following idioms in your own sentences. The first one is done for you.

Idiom : A hot potato
Meaning : An issue (mostly current) which many people are talking about and which is usually disputed
Example : The IPL scam is the *hot potato* for the media across India.

1. Back to the drawing board
2. Blessing in disguise
3. Cry over spilt milk
4. Every cloud has a silver lining
5. Far cry from

V. Use the following phrasal verbs in your own sentences. The first one is done for you.

Phrase : Break out

Meaning : Escape

Example : The prisoners *broke out* of jail when the guards were not looking.

1. Calm down
2. Hang in
3. Put up with
4. Run out
5. Take after

Chapter Ten

Once There Was a King

Rabindranath Tagore

Rabindranath Tagore (1861–1941) *was a poet, artist, playwright, composer and mystic whose work reshaped Bengali literature and music in the late* 19*th and early* 20*th centuries. He became Asia's first Nobel Laureate when he won the* 1913 *Nobel Prize in literature. A prodigious writer, Tagore wrote novels, short stories, dramas and essays on political and personal topics.* Gitanjali, Gora *and* Ghare-Baire *are among his best known works. The national anthem of India,* Jana Mana Gana *was also written by him.*

'Once There was a King' *explores the realm of childhood imagination, fantasy and simple pleasures that can be contrasted with the reality and seriousness of grown-up lives.* 'Once There was a King' *is a story narrated to a young boy. The boy not only lives the story as it is being narrated but unlike adults he can also span over notions of the real and the fantastical with great ease.*

'Once upon a time there was a king.'

When we were children there was no need to know who the king in the fairy story was. It did not matter whether he was called Shiladitya or Shaliban, whether he lived at Kashi or Kannauj. The thing that made a 7-years-old boy's heart go thump, thump with delight was this one sovereign truth, this reality of all realities: 'Once there was a king.'

But the readers of this modern age are far more exact and exacting. When they hear such an opening to a story, they are at once critical and suspicious. They apply the searchlight of science to its legendary haze and ask, 'Which king?'

The storytellers have become more precise in their turn. They are no longer content with the old indefinite, 'There was a king', but assume instead a look of profound learning, and begin, 'Once there was a king named Ajatasatru'.

The modern reader's curiosity, however, is not so easily satisfied. He blinks at the author through his scientific spectacles, and asks again, 'Which Ajatasatru?'

'Every schoolboy knows', the author proceeds, 'that there were three Ajatasatrus. The first was born in the 20th century BC, and died at the tender age of two years and eight months. I deeply regret that it is impossible to find, from any trustworthy source, a detailed account of his reign. The second Ajatasatru is better known to historians, if you refer to the new Encyclopaedia of History.'

By this time the modern reader's suspicions are dissolved. He feels he may safely trust his author. He says to himself, 'Now we shall have a story that is both improving and instructive'.

Ah! how we all love to be deluded! We have a secret dread of being thought ignorant. And we end by being ignorant after all, only we have done it in a long and roundabout way.

There is an English proverb, 'Ask me no questions, and I will tell you no lies'. The boy of seven who is listening to a fairy story understands that perfectly well; he withholds his questions, while the story is being told. So the pure and beautiful falsehood of it all remains naked and innocent as a babe; transparent as truth itself; limpid as a fresh bubbling spring. But the ponderous and learned lie of our moderns has to keep its true character draped and veiled. And if there is discovered anywhere the least little peephole of deception, the reader turns away with a prudish disgust, and the author is discredited.

When we were young, we understood all sweet things; and we could detect the sweets of a fairy story by an unerring science of our own. We never cared for such useless things as knowledge. We only cared for truth.

And our unsophisticated little hearts knew well where the Crystal Palace of Truth lay and how to reach it. But today we are expected to write pages of facts, while the truth is simply this:

'There was a king.'

I remember vividly that evening in Calcutta when the fairy story began. The rain and the storm had been incessant. The whole of the city was flooded. The water was knee-deep in our lane. I had a straining hope, which was almost a certainty, that my tutor would be prevented from coming that evening. I sat on the stool in the far corner of the veranda looking down the lane, with a heart beating faster and faster. Every minute I kept my eye on the rain, and when it began to grow less I prayed with all my might: 'Please, God, send some more rain till half-past seven is over.' For I was quite ready to believe that there was no other need for rain except to protect one helpless boy one evening in one corner of Calcutta from the deadly clutches of his tutor.

If not in answer to my prayer, at any rate according to some grosser law of physical nature, the rain did not give up.

But, alas! Nor did my teacher.

Exactly to the minute, in the bend of the lane, I saw his approaching umbrella. The great bubble of hope burst in my breast, and my heart collapsed. Truly, if there is a punishment to fit the crime after death, then my tutor will be born again as me, and I shall be born as my tutor.

As soon as I saw his umbrella, I ran as hard as I could to my mother's room. My mother and my grandmother were sitting opposite one another playing cards by the light of a lamp. I ran into the room, and flung myself on the bed beside my mother, and said:

'Mother dear, the tutor has come, and I have such a bad headache; couldn't I have no lessons today?'

I hope no child of immature age will be allowed to read this story, and I sincerely trust it will not be used in textbooks or primers for schools. For what I did was dreadfully bad, and I received no punishment whatsoever. On the contrary, my wickedness was crowned with success.

My mother said to me, 'All right', and turning to the servant added, 'Tell the tutor that he can go back home'.

It was perfectly plain that she did not think my illness very serious, as she went on with her game as before, and took no further notice. And I also, burying my head in the pillow, laughed to my heart's content. We perfectly understood one another, my mother and I.

But everyone must know how hard it is for a boy of seven years old to keep up the illusion of illness for long time. After about a minute I got hold of Grandmother, and said, 'Grannie, do tell me a story'.

I had to ask this many times. Grannie and Mother went on playing cards, and took no notice. At last Mother said to me, 'Child, don't bother. Wait till we've finished our game'. But I persisted, 'Grannie, do tell me a story'. I told Mother she could finish her game tomorrow, but she must let Grannie tell me a story there and then.

At last Mother threw down the cards and said, 'You had better do what he wants. I can't manage him'. Perhaps she had it in her mind that she would have no tiresome tutor on the morrow, while I should be obliged to be back to those stupid lessons.

As soon as ever Mother had given way, I rushed at Grannie. I got hold of her hand, and, dancing with delight, dragged her inside my mosquito curtain on to the bed. I clutched hold of the bolster with both hands in my excitement, and jumped up and down with joy, and when I had got a little quieter, said, 'Now, Grannie, let's have the story!'

Grannie went on: 'And the king had a queen.' That was good to begin with. He had only one.

It is usual for kings in fairy stories to be extravagant in queens. And whenever we hear that there are two queens, our hearts begin to sink. One is sure to be unhappy. But in Grannie's story that danger was past. He had only one queen.

We next hear that the king had not got any son. At the age of seven I did not think there was any need to bother if a man had had no son. He might only have been in the way.

Nor are we greatly excited when we hear that the king has gone away into the forest to practice austerities to get a son. There was only one thing that would have made me go into the forest, and that was to get away from my tutor!

But the king left behind with his queen a small girl, who grew up into a beautiful princess.

Twelve years pass away, and the king goes on practicing austerities, and never thinks of his beautiful daughter all this while. The princess has reached the full bloom of her youth. The age of marriage has passed, but the king does not return. And the queen pines away with grief and cries, 'Is my golden daughter destined to die unmarried? Ah me! What a fate is mine'.

Then the queen sent men to the king to entreat him earnestly to come back for a single night and take one meal in the palace. And the king consented.

The queen cooked with her own hand, and with the greatest care, 64 dishes, and made a seat for him of sandalwood, and arranged the food in plates of gold and cups of silver. The princess stood behind with the peacock-tail fan in her hand. The king, after 12 years' absence, came into the house, and the princess waved the fan, lighting up all the room with her beauty. The king looked in his daughter's face, and forgot to take his food.

At last he asked his queen, 'Pray, who is this girl whose beauty shines as the gold image of the goddess? Whose daughter is she?'

The queen beat her forehead, and cried, 'Ah, how evil is my fate! Do you not know your own daughter?'

The king was struck with amazement. He said at last, 'My tiny daughter has grown to be a woman'.

'What else?' the queen said with a sigh. 'Do you not know that 12 years have passed by?'

'But why did you not give her in marriage?' asked the king.

'You were away', the queen said. 'And how could I find her a suitable husband?'

The king became vehement with excitement. 'The first man I see tomorrow', he said, 'when I come out of the palace shall marry her'.

The princess went on waving her fan of peacock feathers, and the king finished his meal.

The next morning, as the king came out of his palace, he saw the son of a Brahman gathering sticks in the forest outside the palace gates. His age was about seven or eight.

The king said, 'I will marry my daughter to him'.

Who can interfere with a king's command? At once the boy was called, and the marriage garlands were exchanged between him and the princess.

At this point, I came up close to my wise Grannie and asked her eagerly, 'What then?'

In the bottom of my heart there was a devout wish to substitute myself for that fortunate wood gatherer of seven years of age. The night was resonant with the patter of rain. The earthen lamp by my bedside was burning low. My grandmother's voice droned on as she told the story. And all these things served to create in a corner of my credulous heart the belief that I had been gathering sticks in the dawn of some indefinite time in the kingdom of some unknown king, and in a moment garlands had been exchanged between me and the princess, beautiful as the Goddess of Grace. She had a gold band on her hair and gold earrings in her ears. She had a necklace and bracelets of gold, and a golden waist chain round her waist, and a pair of golden anklets tinkled above her feet.

If my grandmother were an author how many explanations she would have to offer for this little story! First of all, everyone would ask why the king remained 12 years in the forest? Second, why should the king's daughter have remained unmarried all that while? This would be regarded as absurd.

Even if she could have got so far without a quarrel, still there would have been a great hue and cry about the marriage itself. First, it never happened. Second, how could there be a marriage between a princess of the Warrior caste and a boy of the priestly Brahman caste? Her readers would have imagined at once that the writer was preaching against our social customs in an underhand way. And they would write letters to the papers.

So I pray with all my heart that my grandmother may be born a grandmother again, and not through some cursed fate take birth as her luckless grandson.

So with a throb of joy and delight, I asked Grannie, 'What then?'

Grannie went on: 'Then the princess took her little husband away in great distress, and built a large palace with seven wings, and began to cherish her husband with great care.'

I jumped up and down in my bed and clutched at the bolster more tightly than ever and said, 'What then?'

Grannie continued: 'The little boy went to school and learned many lessons from his teachers, and as he grew up his class fellows began to ask him, "Who is that beautiful lady who lives with you in the palace with the seven wings?"

The Brahman's son was eager to know who she was. He could only remember how one day he had been gathering sticks, and a great disturbance arose. But all that was so long ago that he had no clear recollection.

Four or five years passed in this way. His companions always asked him, "Who is that beautiful lady in the palace with the seven wings?" And the Brahman's son would come back from school and sadly tell the princess, "My school companions always ask me who is that beautiful lady in the palace with the seven wings, and I can give them no reply. Tell me, oh, tell me, who you are!"

The princess said, "Let it pass today. I will tell you some other day". And every day the Brahman's son would ask, "Who are you?" and the princess would reply, "Let it pass today. I will tell you some other day". In this manner four or five more years passed away.

At last the Brahman's son became very impatient, and said, "If you do not tell me today who you are, O beautiful lady, I will leave this palace with the seven wings". Then the princess said, "I will certainly tell you tomorrow".

Next day the Brahman's son, as soon as he came home from school, said, "Now, tell me who you are". The princess said, "Tonight I will tell you after supper, when you are in bed".

The Brahman's son said, "Very well", and he began to count the hours in expectation of the night. And the princess, on her side, spread white flowers over the golden bed, and lighted a gold lamp with fragrant oil, and adorned her hair, and dressed herself in a beautiful robe of blue, and began to count the hours in expectation of the night.

That evening when her husband, the Brahman's son, had finished his meal, too excited almost to eat, and had gone to the golden bed in the bedchamber strewn with flowers, he said to himself, "Tonight I shall surely know who this beautiful lady is in the palace with the seven wings".

The princess took for her the food that was left over by her husband, and slowly entered the bedchamber. She had to answer that night the question, who was the beautiful lady who lived in the palace with the seven wings. And as she went up to the bed to tell him she found a serpent had crept out of the flowers and had bitten the Brahman's son. Her boy husband was lying on the bed of flowers, with face pale in death.'

My heart suddenly ceased to throb, and I asked with choking voice, 'What then?'

Grannie said, 'Then …'

But what is the use of going on any further with the story? It would only lead on to what was more and more impossible. The boy of seven did not know that, if there were some 'What then?' after death, no grandmother of a grandmother could tell us all about it.

But the child's faith never admits defeat, and it would snatch at the mantle of death itself to turn him back. It would be outrageous for him to think that such a story of one teacherless evening could so suddenly come to a stop. Therefore the grandmother had to call back her story from the ever-shut chamber of the great End, but she does it so simply: it is merely by floating the dead body on a banana stem on the river, and having some incantations read by a magician. But in that rainy night and in the dim light of a lamp, death loses all its horror in the mind of the boy and seems nothing more than a deep slumber of a single night. When the story ends the tired eyelids are weighed down with sleep. Thus, it is that we send the little body of the child floating on the back of sleep over the still water of time, and then in the morning read a few verses of incantation to restore him to the world of life and light.

GLOSSARY

Austerities	: Very strict disciplinary habits
Credulous	: Tending to believe things too readily
Deluded	: To be tricked into believing something that is untrue or unreal
Entreat	: To beg somebody for something
Outrageous	: Causing shock or indignation
Precise	: Clear and distinct
Sovereign truth	: Absolute truth
Vehement	: Showing very strong feelings or opinions

COMPREHENSION QUESTIONS

I. Answer the following questions in about one or two words each.

1. What is the name of the king that the story refers to?
2. How many Ajatasatrus were mentioned in the story?
3. How did the king choose a suitor for his daughter?

II. Answer the following questions in about 100–150 words each.

1. Draw a picture of the joy and elation felt by the little boy in the context of the rainy day and being granted permission to miss his tuition class.
2. Why did the mother give up her game and ask Grannie to tell the boy a story? Comment on the mother's attitude.
3. Why did the king in the fairy tale go away to the forest? What was his experience when he returned after 12 years?
4. Why do you think the fairy tale can only be a fairy tale and not a real story?
5. What happens to the princess after her marriage?
6. What is the fantastical ending woven by Grannie for the fairy tale?
7. Comment on the author's use of poetic language to tell his story.

III. Answer the following questions in about 200–250 words each.

1. Draw out instances from the story to illustrate the precept that children live more intensely than adults.

IV. Use the following idioms in your own sentences. The first one is done for you.

Idiom : Work like a charm
Meaning : Works very well or has the desired effect
Example : I had cloves for my sore throat, and they *worked like a charm.*

1. Get a grip on yourself
2. Golden handshake
3. Have on the brain
4. Have one's heart set on
5. Mean business
6. Not let grass grow under feet

7. Sink your teeth into
8. Waiting in the wings

V. Use the following phrasal verbs in your own sentences. The first one is done for you.

Phrasal verb : Hang on
Meaning : Wait
Example : *Hang on* a minute. I'm almost ready.

1. Bank on
2. Drop behind
3. Get rid of
4. Hook up
5. Make fun of
6. Name after
7. Set off
8. Tear up

Literary Credits

Chapter 3: Extract reprinted from the Nobel Lecture "*Let Us Globalise Compassion, and Set Our Children Free*" by Kailash Satyarthi, with permission. Copyright © The Nobel Foundation 2014.

Chapter 7: Extract reprinted from the *The Doctor's Word* by R.K. Narayan with permission. Copyright © Legal heirs of R.K. Narayan.